SALES
MANAGEMENT
SUCCESS

Hi ELIZABETH,
BEST WISHES FOR
YOUR CONTINUED
MANAGEMENT SUCCESS.

Warren Kurzrock

SALES

OPTIMIZING PERFORMANCE

TO BUILD

MANAGEMENT

A POWERFUL

SALES TEAM

SUCCESS

WARREN KURZROCK, CEO, PORTER HENRY & CO., INC.

WILEY

Published by John Wiley & Sons, Inc., Hoboken, New Jersey.
Published simultaneously in Canada.

For general information on our other products and services or for technical support, please contact our Customer Care Department within the United States at (800) 762-2974, outside the United States at (317) 572-3993 or fax (317) 572-4002.

Wiley publishes in a variety of print and electronic formats and by print-on-demand. Some material included with standard print versions of this book may not be included in e-books or in print-on-demand. If this book refers to media such as a CD or DVD that is not included in the version you purchased, you may download this material at http://booksupport.wiley.com. For more information about Wiley products, visit www.wiley.com.

Library of Congress Cataloging-in-Publication Data:

Names: Kurzrock, Warren, author.
Title: Sales management success : optimizing performance to build a powerful sales team / Warren Kurzrock, CEO, Porter Henry & Co., Inc.
Description: Hoboken, New Jersey : John Wiley & Sons, Inc., [2020] | Includes index. |
Identifiers: LCCN 2019011597 (print) | LCCN 2019013698 (ebook) | ISBN 9781119575917 (Adobe PDF) | ISBN 9781119575856 (ePub) | ISBN 9781119575924 (hardcover)
Subjects: LCSH: Sales management.
Classification: LCC HF5438.4 (ebook) | LCC HF5438.4 .K869 2020 (print) | DDC 658.8/1—dc23

LC record available at https://lccn.loc.gov/2019011597

Cover Design: Wiley

Printed in the United States of America

V10013292_082319

CONTENTS

PREFACE

Sales Management Success offers huge value to every current and potential sales manager, regardless of experience or future ambitions. It contains advanced, sophisticated, researched "how to" content and all of the strategies, processes, and ideas have "Monday morning applicability." For the majority of sales managers, it will kick-start new dimensions of sales leadership, add break-through solutions, and provide exclusive strategies for each sales manager's success and that of the sales team.

Three exclusive benefits validate the book's value:

1. Proven, State-of-the-Art Content

    The book contains tested strategies and abilities developed by Porter Henry & Co. over the past 75 years. Thousands of companies from Fortune 500 to small independents have invested heavily to train their sales managers via Porter Henry workshops and have gained sales management success. Equally important, participating companies have shared experiences and contributed countless ideas that are incorporated in the workshop curriculum and the book's content.

2. Tested Content, Current Research

Considerable research was done to enhance the existing content in terms of studies, workshop development, current data and analysis, documented experience, and research by others. While a few of the strategies have existed in different content and formats, the eight strategies featured here are Porter Henry & Co. exclusive. New ones have emerged as a result of research and development including strategic abilities for: "Aligning, Enhancing Sales Motivation," "Virtual Sales Coaching," "Sales Leadership Vision," the STAR Questioning Process (interviewing), and "ROI Decision-Making."

3. A Sales Manager Development Program

The book is unique in that it is literally a training program; it includes a Toolbox (Chapter 10) with 13 tools and instructions to capitalize on the eight strategies. Designed and written by a successful sales manager, sales trainer, top sales executive, and thought leader, the book is organized around the vital strategies needed to guarantee a sales manager's success. Since a strategy is ongoing, and often long-term, each strategy includes a rationale, necessary planning, key steps, how to implement it with the sales team, and application tools for making it work successfully. As a sales manager training program, the book covers goals, self-development, application, and the skills and abilities required to drive each strategy.

INTRODUCTION

NO SALES OR MARKETING EXECUTIVE will dispute the importance of the frontline sales manager/sales leader. Yet much has been said, argued, and written about the difference between being a "sales manager" or a "sales leader." In simple terms, there is *no difference* between the two titles/positions. However, the sales leader position is the ultimate achievement for the developing sales manager. The jobs per se are largely related, overlapping subjects to company salesforce expectations, but accomplished with more perfection and success by a frontline sales manager leading the sales team effectively, rather than just managing performance. The sales leader, with greater skills, ability, and vision, is the ultimate person to both manage daily activity, and equally important, lead his sales team followers on a long-term path to sustained success.

This book will further define the overlapping sales manager/sales leader position(s) and challenges, along with how to develop the essential strategies and skills required for success. It also provides a strategic foundation and development plan for every future sales manager or leader. This promise is based on Porter Henry & Co.'s 75 years of research, development, and training provided for tens of thousands of salespeople and sales managers/leaders. It obviously includes my personal experiences with Porter Henry, and previous success as a salesperson, frontline sales manager, sales trainer consultant, and CEO. The book covers the most impactful sales manager/leadership strategies and accompanying skills, some of which have not been available in any format previously (except Porter Henry & Co. workshops). This book will not deal with core essentials like personality, industry and product knowledge, analytical ability, and business acumen, based on the assumption that they are inherent or developed normally through education and work experience.

Sales Management Success is dedicated to salespeople who are motivated to become managers and to sales managers determined to improve and become the ultimate sales leader. Corporate sales executives and sales trainers will also find a plethora of ideas and tools for developing their own sales managers. This book will support every reader's sales manager/leader ambitions. Keep in mind, however, Malcolm Gladwell's profound research in his best-selling *Outliers* book that states, "If you practice anything for a minimum of 10,000 hours you will become an expert." He cites many professionals who have achieved success with the 10,000-hour rule. Professional sales leadership fits in this rule, and is also a long, challenging journey, but the rewards and satisfaction transcend the lengthy time investment and efforts to develop on the job.

As you will learn, if you don't know it already, growth and progress, driven by strategy, supported by skills and ability development (and success, of course) parallel a marathon. It is a great analogy for achieving sales leadership.

I ran my first of two New York City marathons after never previously running more than three miles. The marathons were relatively easy, but a six-month strategy of daily training was tough and excruciating, working up to running 20 miles once a week in preparation for the 26.2-mile challenge. It took many steps, required adding a mile each week to get there, as part of the training strategy.

While I didn't have a book in mind at the time, it now becomes a perfect analogy for the ambitious sales leader-to-be. As a former sales manager, and sales leader, I now see the similarity and track as almost identical. Reading the book won't take long, including studying some of the content, gaining feedback (with a few assessments), and using the tools, but acquiring the skills and knowledge to be a better sales manager, moving to sales leader, will be lengthy, certainly more than the hours needed to read this book, or months to train and complete a marathon.

Each step is vital and will give you satisfaction when achieved, and motivation to move to the next one. Running a marathon like this is not easy, but the achievement, in terms of the successful performance and new abilities, transcend the pain. Hopefully, you will visualize this book, as well as study and use it as your marathon path to ultimate sales leadership success.

Great selling, managing, leading, and success … in your growing career!

Cheers,
Warren Kurzrock, CEO, Porter Henry & Co., Inc.

Download Your Complimentary Digital Toolbox

An expanded, usable version of Your Turbo-Charged Toolbox (Chapter 10), with the 13 tools, instructions, and examples, is available for *Sales Management Success* book buyers. This digital version will enable you to customize the tools, copy them, and add them to your computer for on-the-job use. The only restriction is that the Porter Henry & Co., Inc. copyright must remain on all copies. **To acquire your personal copy**, visit porterhenry.com and click Strategic Sales Manager Toolbox on the home page to open the Shop page. Complete the required information, insert the coupon code ACHIEVE, and download your free copy.

SALES MANAGEMENT SUCCESS

1

How Eight Interacting Strategies Drive Synergistic Success

THE SALES MANAGER POSITION is the most challenging in the salesforce, possibly on the planet. I've been there and done that, and can vouch for its challenges. That's why 50% of new sales managers fail within the first two years! This book will enable every sales manager to become more successful with accompanying rewards, glory, and satisfaction. Most sales managers are enthusiastic, hard-working, and love the job, yet they recognize the pain and challenges that handicap results. The book is for experienced sales leaders, rookie sales managers, top sales executives, sales trainers, ambitious salespeople dreaming of promotion, and students with sales management learning objectives.

Most sales managers supervise a team of 5–10 salespeople who act like "Lone Rangers" targeting accounts to achieve sales quota. They often lack proximity to the sales manager, operate on their own, are driven by different motivations, sell to unique prospects/customers, have a range of skill levels, unique personalities, individual behaviors. Bringing each to 100% quota is a huge job in itself, but most sales managers struggle in a chaotic environment of interruptions, hiring and firing surges, finding time to accomplish slippery priorities, handling customer problems, driving hard to satisfy management pressure.

Every sales manager certainly recognizes the dynamics and demands of the job and the challenge of accomplishing more in less time to achieve goals. However, success cannot be gained with the huge number of tasks, challenges, pace, emergencies, and a widespread sales team if goals and actions are managed piecemeal. Strategies to the rescue! Most sales managers crave a more organized, efficient process, and it can only be accomplished with strategic applications.

As you may know, a strategy is long-term; starts with a goal, planning, a process, and steps; provides a track to run on; and offers an organized solution. The eight strategies in this book, which often overlap, can solve the sales manager's biggest problems and enhance overall leadership. The words "Turbo-Charged" in the title promise that the strategies have speed, efficiency, power, and significant values to help drive your success and that of your sales team.

This book is not a magic formula for doing the sales manager's job. But it is an added guarantee for professional success. Learning the strategies will help you organize, target, and accomplish high-value priorities, use new ideas, tools, and skills that go hand-in-hand with each strategy. They also demand that you improve some skills and abilities in order to make them work.

These eight exclusive strategies have evolved from Porter Henry & Co.'s 75 years of research, training tens of thousands of sales managers and salespeople, and my own successful sales manager/sales training experience. Each chapter, except this one and the last (your Toolbox) contains one or more strategies designed for targeted, ongoing application as a dynamic process with accompanying tools to keep you on track and avoid the daily traps. The book is literally your exclusive sales manager course, in easy-learning format, to enhance your success. These strategies will help you stay organized, enable you to capitalize on your talents, keep on track, dramatically achieve your goals and increase your sales team's performance.

NO ONE EVER SAID THE SALES MANAGER JOB IS EASY

This book is about positive solutions, but before I get into the strategies and their successful application, it's important to look at both sides of the job and fully recognize the challenges the strategies help you overcome. Ask any first-line sales manager about his or her job and you'll quickly learn that it's the "best" but most challenging of all positions. The rewards are usually great because they are based on the sales manager's performance. The opportunity is huge, and the sales manager is responsible for revenue, and often profits. The dream side of the job offers visibility, recognition, and reasonable freedom from headquarters' intrusions.

On the down side, it's one of the most challenging, difficult, and frustrating positions in today's salesforce. In spite of being the most critical job in the salesforce, the pain is exacerbated by a variety of interacting obstacles and traps. Unfortunately, top sales executives, who once were the first-line managers, quickly forget what it was like in the trenches and usually fail to recognize that the key to sales is not the sales team, but the manager who drives it.

Gary Hardy, former sales executive leader for the DOW Chemical Company, clearly defines the importance of the first-line sales manager:

> The key to a high-performance sales force is the first-line sales manager. It's inevitably the first-line sales manager who communicates expectations, directly or indirectly provides the knowledge and skills to succeed, actively provides the coaching and counseling needed to overcome obstacles and barriers, and rewards based upon the degree to which expectations are met. To effectively develop a world-class sales team, you must first come to grips with the critical and multi-faceted role played by the sales manager. And, it should immediately become clear that the transition from Player to Coach is full of dangerous misconceptions. If you don't address the skill gaps that were never tested as a Player, they will quickly swallow both the new Coach and your sales results.

WHERE IS THE PAIN?

In most cases, the first-line sales manager lacks proximity to the majority of his team, so salespeople and account managers operate out of sight most of the time. Spotty supervision, coaching, and management are performed on the run via email and telephone, and are supplemented with infrequent, task-packed visits. This is not a very good scenario for determining who needs help, who's fully motivated, who's struggling. With a large span of control, it's an awesome job to drive successful team performance, often with an overwhelming workload of headquarter and customer problems.

The "devil" is in the salesperson, as well. Most salespeople are reasonably independent, aggressive, risk-taking, confident, high-energy people. Consequently, the good ones are on the move and often reluctant to ask for help. To compound the challenge, they are all special—diverse personalities, varying experiences, different motivations, and personal needs. Each sales rep operates in a territory or account segment that is unique. Ostensibly the sales team members perform the same job, but the above characteristics and other factors make each salesperson remarkably different.

Unfortunately, management often takes a cavalier attitude about the sales manager job. At 40,000 feet (in the executive tower) the waves on the beach look flat, but on the sand, they're often huge, breaking over the head of the sales manager with a resounding crash. This lack of awareness is extreme for the newly promoted first-line sales manager. As a result, most sales manager learning is done on the job, or at a three- to four-day orientation focusing on procedures and products. There are a number of reasons for this: many successful sales organizations delay formal training (since they often promote one manager or a few at a time), send the manager off to a generic management course (with nonsales executives who have different problems and issues), or neglect her altogether. The bottom line according to the Association for Talent Development (ATD) is that only 11% of companies offer their sales managers extensive training.

The popular feeling is that the job is largely intuitive, and since most first-line sales managers are promoted from the sales ranks, they should have a good feel for the job and the capability to grow into it. Nothing could be further from the truth. The best salespeople—managers-to-be—often shoot from the hip (albeit accurately); are risk-takers, comfortable managing themselves and their accounts; have strong selling and relationship skills, soft or no analytical, supervisory, management, and administrative skills. As indicated earlier, they are suddenly placed in a chaotic, strange environment and challenged to manage people, events, plans, and problems. Even proven sales managers hired from outside the company offer huge risks without the proper orientation and ongoing training.

While it's imperative to grasp the big picture, most sales managers are reactionary and busy. They don't have the ability or time to drill down to the "subway" level and determine what's really causing a problem or situation. Instead, they jump into action to rescue the failing salesperson (often too late) before he goes down the proverbial drainpipe.

Quite often, in the need for speed, sales managers focus on revenue rather than performance symptoms (actual causes) and identify a problem when it's beyond correction.

_____

THE INDIVIDUAL CHALLENGE TO BECOME A SALES LEADER

In spite of the huge obstacles, there are solutions that provide management with all the improved results: sales growth, minimum sales team turnover, and a deep bench for developing future sales executives (sales leaders!). The job of first-line sales manager needs a mandate: "train to relieve the pain." While some salesforce positions can get by with standard or even mediocre training, the complexity of the key sales manager position, and challenges described, require—demand—the ultimate in sales manager development. The cookbook recipe is simple to comprehend, but difficult to execute, and should be an ongoing challenge/priority supported by:

- Leading-edge content: strategies, tools, skills, abilities, processes
- Continuous learning and practice to apply concepts, exchange ideas
- Access to timely sales data, along with ongoing coaching, reinforcement
- Constant follow-up to ensure that strategies and skills are applied correctly and improvements are being made

This book will provide world-class strategies and "how to" ideas, but you are the only person who can apply these concepts to your job, and work toward becoming the ultimate sales leader that you deserve.

Doug Willner, director of training for Medimmune, Inc., underlined the challenge:

Typically managerial training seems to be secondary to the product, or disease training. We have prioritized a consistent schedule and process for continuous learning and reinforcement for our managers to ensure that their own skill development is maintained at the highest level. Our managers are trained in advance of their teams and provided with reinforcement and coaching tools so they are able to effectively assess and provide critical feedback to their teams. We are sending a clear message that their managerial and leadership skills are every bit as important as the product knowledge.

There are many critical sales manager abilities, competencies, and skills (possibly as many as 20) that interact together to provide a solution. Together, these abilities enable the first-line sales managers to stay in control and manage themselves, their people, their customers, account problems, and to become true leaders. Keep in mind that development is the individual's responsibility no matter where he or she solicits learning or direction. This book is an exclusive place to identify, define, and learn today's most critical strategies, but they need to be learned, applied, and supported with skills and abilities that only you can contribute.

OVERVIEW OF THE EIGHT STRATEGIES

Following is a brief overview of the eight strategies, including the Toolbox in Chapter 10 that contains 13 vital instruments for application. While the strategies are each separate in the chapters of this book, keep in mind that they all interact in real life to create synergistic success for your sales team.

The Dynamic Duo Sales Coaching Strategy (Chapter 2)

Sales coaching is an essential skill for any first-line manager, and training-oriented companies focus on it with passion. Rightfully so. However, a major global study generated by the renowned Sales Executive Council concluded: (1) without on-the-job reinforcement, reps lose 87% of training within one month, and (2) although many companies recognize the importance of coaching and do a reasonable job of coaching training, they often overlook the fact that sales managers spend less than 10% of time in the field.

Depending on the size of the sales team, the 10% max means that the average coach will visit each rep one or two times a year. Hardly worth the trips! However, the dynamic duo sales coaching strategy includes "virtual sales coaching," which will dramatically improve coaching quality and specifically multiply frequency of coaching. The "dynamic duo," field + virtual coaching, along with unique tools and methods become a powerful strategy that will enable you to significantly improve sales team performance.

A Strategy for Managing Sales Performance (Chapter 3)

The accepted method for managing the sales team is to review revenue numbers on a monthly or quarterly basis and zero in on the less-than-quota-pace performers; unfortunately, the data is limited and often 30–60 days late; forecasts are often unreliable. Enlightened companies or creative sales managers devise systems for monitoring key performance indicators (KPI) like calls made, product mix sold, frequency of sales calls on major accounts, strategy execution, and yes, even selling skills—is each salesperson improving, vegetating, plateauing?

This chapter and strategy provide a managing sales performance process and cadence for tracking KPIs that will enable the sales manager to continuously review ongoing performance actions/behaviors that improve performance, rather than trying to save "souls" when the numbers are down at the end of the quarter. The benefit of a good strategy and knowing how to use it enables you to recognize performance "warning signs and symptoms" early on, *before* they become big problems.

Counseling Strategy for Attitude and Performance Problems (Chapter 4)

Counseling is a management process designed to deal with attitude, motivation, and performance problems (i.e., where coaching doesn't work). Unfortunately, counseling is often confused with coaching. In simple terms, coaching is used for skill development, where counseling is employed to handle individual problems. It's a great tool for understanding each person's needs and goals, as well as what motivates a salesperson to perform better.

Counseling can be used in a positive way to help the sales leader support each salesperson's desire to reach peak performance. Often triggered by a performance problem, counseling enables the sales leader to connect in-depth with an individual. Most important, it helps the sales leader determine causes of problems and solutions, and to develop a long-term plan of improvement. The counseling strategy can also be employed to communicate and reinforce individual progress or a significant win.

Optimizing Time to Achieve Priorities Strategy (Chapter 5)

With all the obstacles in the work life of the time-challenged frontline sales manager, you'd think that most sales organizations would elevate priority-time management as a top-level need for their sales leaders. Yet there are few opportunities for development in this strategy, and most are short-term Band-Aids. That's why the strategy, process, skills, and discipline covered in this chapter are vital for any sales manager who wants to transcend to sales leader and accomplish much more.

Priority and time management are more than an instinctive process. The common assumption is that if you give a manager a daily planner or Microsoft Outlook, she can figure it out for herself. Not so. Strategic planning and skills are needed. In terms of productivity and efficiency, priority/time management therefore ranks high in managing and sustaining both daily and ongoing performance. This strategy will enable you to identify your priorities and make sure they get sufficient time for completion. It will also help you avoid or manage a multitude of time-wasters that subtly absorb your productive time.

A Strategy to Improve Team Selling Skills, and Yours! (Chapter 6)

You may be surprised that I am including a strategy on selling skill development in a book on sales management and leadership. My rationale is simple. No matter how much sales experience—or high sales success—you have had, as a sales leader you must have a 100% grasp of current, advanced sales skills and strategies for every situation. In addition to help winning the sale, as sales leader, you need to build and maintain respect from your sales team. Regardless of whether you are coaching, developing an account strategy, hiring, assessing performance, or any related activity, you should provide the best sales/strategy advice or model 100% of the time. As sales manager you are the #1 sales expert and you can't rely on past experience alone.

This chapter will provide a review of seven key sales skills and strategies. Equally important, it will test your skills and give you access to an online measurement tool, Porter Henry's Sales*Pro* Performance Indicator (SPI) so you can actually measure and score your current sales skill strengths and knowledge.

Strategies to Align and Enhance Sales Motivation (Chapter 7)

Every sales executive talks about the importance of motivation or having "mojo" as a requirement for success. Motivation, however, is almost a mystery, since we're all unique, and the many motives can change rapidly. What we do know for sure:

- All salespeople are motivated to sell, and the challenge is often getting them to raise the level or shift their focus.

- As sales manager, you don't motivate your salespeople since no one really motivates anyone else; however, you can impact motivation and performance by understanding the concept and offering subtle options to awaken or reinforce it.

- There are many motivations, all difficult to read because they are personal, intangible, and hidden, and of course, each salesperson is different.

In spite of the challenges, you can enable and support a salesperson's individual motivation by (1) understanding the big picture of motivation, providing reinforcement, and (2) launching two exclusive strategies based on current motivational research, Mastery and Autonomy; if offered to team members for their development, either or both can lead to enhanced motivation and improved sales performance.

The Strategy for Hiring Future Sales Stars (Chapter 8)

While HR, recruiting sources, and upper sales management can influence selection and share in it, the ultimate decision should be that of the frontline sales leader. The sales manager will unconsciously abandon this role unless he is totally equipped with confidence and training to make the decision or significantly influence the final selection. After all, who knows more about the needs of customers, demands of the territory, the characteristics needed to maintain a relationship, and fit with the rest of the sales team, than the sales leader?

With many salesforces facing a costly annual turnover of 10–50%, a proven hiring strategy is a significant advantage (rather than a challenge, often populated with hiring mistakes). You will learn how to avoid mistakes, reduce future turnover, and optimize your selections to benefit the sales team and needs of the territory. This unique strategy will offer many ideas, methods, and tools to hire future sales stars.

Strategizing for the Ultimate Sales Leader (Chapter 9)

As mentioned earlier, I recognize a difference between a sales manager and a sales leader, although the titles are interchangeable, and basically, they do the same job. Based on my experience, the typical frontline sales manager focuses mostly on daily activities, employing her abilities to execute the strategies and tasks described earlier. The ultimate sales leader, however, finds time and uses his ability to zero in on long-term sales team performance, fast-forwarding his vision to the future. This requires a master strategy driven by interacting personal abilities.

While the previous strategies offer a critical foundation, this chapter will embrace the added sales leader performance. This zeros in on your abilities in leading your sales team long term, while establishing yourself as their true leader. The path to becoming the ultimate sales leader includes these overlapping strategies:

- *Strategic vision*—The ability to identify opportunities and develop plans and strategies that lead, unite, and drive your sales team in one direction to complete successful campaigns.
- *Decision-making*—The capability to make the right decisions with a high "batting average" to achieve success and earn "followers'" respect from your sales team.
- *Influence*—Influencing your sales team is critical and usually accomplished through communication: your personal style of communicating based on the situation, or personal abilities like building trust, being a role model.

Your Turbo-Charged Strategic Toolbox (Chapter 10)

The Toolbox helps validate this book as a "course" since it provides 13 tools with instructions for in-field application. While the book introduces these tools as examples for specific strategy execution, the Toolbox organizes them together with instructions for use and application with your sales team.

This book is for reading, but I hope you will value this as a personal development program, employing the content, ideas, tools, and feedback to optimize your development as a sales leader. You will find each chapter is literally a short course in itself, one that can set the stage for targeted development and inspire you to apply the skills and abilities successfully with your sales team. Hopefully, it will help you stay on track as you run a marathon to become the ultimate sales leader.

2

The Dynamic Duo Sales
Coaching Strategy

JOE AMES WAS AN experienced sales rep, a star hire, and his potential was recognized during onboarding and training. His sales manager was also impressed with his basic sales skills during her early field coaching sessions. Joe was fearless, great at prospecting, and a strong presenter. However, he needed work on his probing skills to identify applications, surface detailed needs, and overcome objections to the high cost of their system. The sales manager planned to visit Joe one or two times a month to coach and reinforce skills, but other job demands limited her to three coaching visits in the first nine months. Joe left at the end of his first year, frustrated, demotivated, at 55% of annual first-year quota.

This sales manager's main problem was coaching frequency, a global shortcoming underlined by studies pinpointing coaching time at less than 10%! Overloaded with tasks and demands created by nine salespeople, she hoped Joe's potential would help him develop. Frequency is the #1 coaching challenge for today's sales managers.

Every smart sales manager knows field coaching is a priority. Unfortunately, the time available is literally locked at less than 10%, and there has been no remedy in sight for most sales managers ... until now. The dynamic duo strategy, field + virtual sales coaching, provides a proven coaching process and skills, and the bottom-line value is quadrupling coaching frequency to adequately reinforce/correct individual skill performance.

COACHING FREQUENCY IS THE #1 CHALLENGE

Many sales managers currently coach in either a "routing" method, visiting each person with same frequency, or a "crisis" mode, on-demand to rescue a failing rep, or to close a big deal. Both methods limit and contradict the coaching objective, since they focus on the wrong people, a rep who is destined to fail, or one who really doesn't need help.

The field coaching part of the strategy provides a proven, unique process for allocating coaching time for the best ROI; it uses tools to measure both "need for coaching" and "coachability." (Why waste time on a rigid person who resists change?) Virtual sales coaching, which enables the sales manager to coach from anywhere, anytime, dramatically increases coaching frequency while supporting field coaching efforts. Both must work together as part of the strategy in order to complement each other and optimize performance improvement.

If you're like most sales managers, you recognize the importance of sales coaching, and enjoy it, yet are frustrated with how little time is available for coaching your sales team in the field. Traditional field coaching, done on a one-to-one basis periodically with salespeople, is the ideal way to coach; it enables the manager to observe what is being done effectively and helps the sales manager improve skill/knowledge gaps and reinforce what each sales rep is doing well. While some companies, and some industries, allow (or insist!) the sales manager to work frequently in the field, the majority have overloaded today's sales manager with many tasks and expanded sales teams, thus limiting vital field coaching time (and results!).

The good news is, according to a study by TrainingIndustry.com, retention is 65% higher with coaching than with just training. In addition, Google's Project Oxygen Study has shown that coaching is the number one key behavior for good managers. Improving the frequency of coaching is a huge challenge along with how to determine your allocation of coaching among your sales team members. And of course, providing top-quality, effective coaching is essential. Assuming you get the message about the importance of sales coaching and an optimized frequency for visits, here's how to accomplish coaching objectives that contribute greatly to your sales team's success.

THE SALES COACHING DYNAMIC DUO

Recognizing the frequency shortfall in traditional field coaching, virtual sales coaching was created to eliminate the huge gap. Porter Henry Co. can take credit for its development and as far as I can see, we offer the only comprehensive virtual sales coaching experience globally. While coaching skills are important, the bottom-line coaching challenge, in simple terms, is coaching *frequency*. At 10% time allocation for coaching, you probably visit each team member once or twice a year—bad news for new or struggling reps, missing motivation and ideas for the experienced team members.

As a former sales rep, or sales manager now, do you think coaching twice a year is really helpful? Not so much. Coaching, to be effective, not only needs to be fairly frequent with little time between visits, but it must be focused on one or two skills or behaviors so you don't give the salesperson indigestion from too much learning at one time. In my early days as a branch manager, I was so eager to succeed that I took copious notes on every coaching call, covering multiple skills or tactics that could be improved. This technique ended for me very suddenly, when one bright sales rep responded to my coaching critique by saying: "Whoa! I can't swallow all of this stuff at one time. What was the main thing I failed to do, or did poorly, that would have made this sale?" Amen.

While field sales coaching per se may be limited these days, it still provides huge value. The sales manager can view the salesperson firsthand, to see him perform, and then coach immediately after each call to both reinforce or upgrade performance while details are fresh in both minds. Field sales coaching is also vital for the manager's credibility and sales rep's motivation (attention and support) and ideally sets the stage for identifying realistic development objectives for each salesperson. As indicated, its main shortcoming is lack of frequency, since coaching trips usually involve one or two days, require travel time and costs, and are limited to visiting accounts in reasonable driving proximity to each other. Bottom-line: field sales coaching is a "must" as a foundation for virtual sales coaching, and as a periodic checkup on "real-world" individual progress.

Virtual sales coaching, the new partner in the dynamic duo coaching strategy, not only fills the field coaching frequency gap but adds benefits of its own. By definition, it means the sales manager can coach the sales team members at any time or from anywhere, since most of it is done by phone with email support. Above all, its frequency is unlimited, so coaching can be handled with each individual as often as needed. It takes less time, since the manager won't be traveling or joining the salesperson on the call, and enables holding the coaching session at a convenient time for both parties. The main benefit, as indicated, is frequency, but another significant plus is that it allows the sales manager and salesperson to target specific accounts (anywhere) since the sales manager's travel and timeline, to accompany the salesperson, are not issues.

Virtual sales coaching has limitations, primarily gaining in-depth, objective feedback from the sales rep in a timely fashion for coaching. Your virtual challenge is learning to coach a presentation that you did not witness firsthand. Later you will learn how benefits and challenges are accomplished to make virtual sales coaching and field coaching the ideal duo for sales performance improvement.

Finally, this strategy will focus on a third skill, allocating coaching among members of the sales team. It's important to determine who gets coached most frequently, and which team members deserve less coaching. Allocating coaching time and "visits" helps you optimize the coaching activity for your team and provide the best payback in terms of results and use of your time. Here's a more in-depth look at the dynamic sales coaching duo, starting with the field coaching strategy segment.

FIELD COACHING

Sales managers love to coach because, for many of them, it's a return to selling, what they do best. Some are so enthused that they often take over the presentation or get involved, rather than observing. Not a good habit. Field coaching is a process with a number of critical steps and guidelines to make it work effectively. In simple terms, it requires observing a sales call, and coaching afterward based on what you have seen and heard. Obviously there are many steps and pitfalls that will be covered in this chapter. Let's start with the first step, the pre-call briefing.

The Pre-call Briefing

To ensure that your post-call coaching will work, it is imperative that you spend a few minutes with the salesperson immediately prior to the sales call, developing both a tactical plan and a coaching regimen. Five minutes invested in a briefing will bring you up to date on the account, enable you to check the salesperson's game plan or strategy, and determine your role during the presentation. It sets the stage for your observation and will improve the quality of the sales call and enhance the coaching afterward. It will also help you determine how much preplanning the sales rep has done, and even enable you to do some pre–sales call coaching based on the feedback. If working on a specific development plan for the rep, you can reinforce the skill you want to focus on and prepare her for the coaching afterward.

Make sure your pre-call briefing includes the following:

- *Have salesperson describe the account's history* and current status.
- *Discuss his call objective* and game plan for the sales call, reviewing potential obstacles and strategy.
- *Explain your coaching focus* for this specific call. If appropriate, describe the skills, knowledge, or behaviors that you'll be observing.
- *Determine the roles* you'll play. In most cases, you should be observing. But there may be some segments that you will want to handle for demonstration purposes. This part of the briefing should also determine signals for "rescuing" if problems arise. With rookies it's a good idea to use an informal role-play prior to the call to prep the salesperson, enhance his confidence, and to set the stage for success.

The pre-call briefing is extremely valuable in learning the rep's planning and understanding of the situation, and it will set the stage for a productive presentation and effective coaching afterward.

Field Coaching Process

Field coaching is a process that enables the sales manager to observe the salesperson in a live customer or prospect situation and conduct a "curbstone conference" immediately after while details are fresh. As mentioned earlier, it is the ideal way to train after basic learning, or at any time, and while limited today because of challenging coaching frequency, it has a powerful role in every salesperson's development. As part of the "dynamic duo," field coaching sets the foundation while virtual sales coaching provides the critical follow-up, reinforcement, and sustainable development field until the next visit.

Your observation is key, which means that if you expect to coach afterward, you cannot have a big selling role. I know it's tough to stay out of the presentation, especially if you have had a significant sales record. Recognize that no one sells like you and some will do better, and discipline yourself to be an observer. In my coaching days, I had the sales rep introduce me as an associate, rather than a branch manager, traveling along for the day, which minimized the customer's attention on me. Obviously, this is not always possible in accounts where the customer knows you. Remember—if this is a coaching sales call, fade into the woodwork when possible, and quietly observe. If you get dragged into the presentation with a question, quickly answer it, and pass the ball back to your salesperson.

Most important, field coaching is a process, not a series of inflexible steps. After observing a sales call, the process drives a positive discussion, it reinforces what the salesperson is doing well, and focuses on improving skills and knowledge that surface during the presentation. The field coaching process is triggered by a post-call discussion, which may only take a few minutes as soon as possible after the call. It may not be necessary to employ all of the coaching techniques and you should avoid using the same order each time. Employing the process in the same way during every coaching discussion would make the process too predictable and mechanical. A professional coaching process will include these techniques or tactics (again, not steps!), but some coaching discussions may not require them all, and certainly you should avoid always following the same specific order:

- Reinforce positive behavior.
- Have salesperson analyze the call.
- Use leading questions.
- Suggest a better way.
- Elicit feedback.
- Encourage practice using the skill.
- Get commitment.

Let's expand on these essential coaching techniques. While I will follow this order, as mentioned, it's a good idea to mix it up, add your own thoughts and personality, and give lots of feedback, hopefully positive. In some instances you may be better off skipping some of the techniques or bypassing the coaching altogether by providing a sincere compliment, or specific skill reinforcement, before moving to the next call.

Reinforce Positive Behavior

Based on your observation, reinforce the skill or behavior(s) that was performed well so that the salesperson will know to continue and repeat the skill effectively on future calls. A positive beginning often sets the tone for the remainder of the conference. Ideally, it will be an agreed-upon skill that you and the salesperson are focusing on improving. Positive reinforcement should meet the following guidelines:

- *Be specific*—so that the salesperson knows for sure the skill behaviors to repeat and the ones to eliminate.
- *Use reinforcement promptly*—such as immediately as the call is discussed, to make sure that it is not delayed (and forgotten).
- *Maintain proper frequency of reinforcement*—reinforce each occurrence of a new or improved behavior but also recognize that behaviors that are fairly well established and just need to be slightly improved do not always need reinforcement.

Make your reinforcement words count. Simply saying, "That was a great call. Congratulations!" may make the salesperson feel good and keep her motivated, but this does little for reinforcement. Specific reinforcement sounds like this: "You really handled that pricing objection well, particularly indicating a discount would be provided if the customer ordered in larger quantities. Keep it up."

Have Salesperson Analyze the Call

One of the major goals of coaching is to help your salespeople learn how to evaluate and improve their own performance when you're not there. Asking the salesperson to analyze his or her performance has the following benefits:

- It encourages self-coaching and reinforces the fact that the salesperson should be analyzing each call.

- You learn how much the salesperson knows about sales technique, product knowledge, applications, and so on.
- The salesperson might point out performance areas that you were planning to discuss, or that you dismissed as less important.
- A salesperson is likely to be more committed to taking action to solve problems that he or she uncovers.
- Most important, it's democratic, builds relationships, and encourages the salesperson's valuable input, which can offer clues as to motivation, rationale, and maybe some ideas that you, the sales manager, had not thought of.

Use Leading Questions

In coaching, where you rely on getting agreement, questioning is critical. There may be times when there's a conflict between your analysis and that of the salesperson. He may think part of the call went perfectly; you may see the need for improvement. On the other hand, she may not be able to cite positive aspects readily; you may have one or more strong points in mind. In cases like this you can get the person to "discover" a development need or strength by using specific leading questions like these:

- "Do you recall what you said when the customer brought up leasing ... ?"
- "Were you comfortable with the way you presented our efficiency benefits?"
- "How could your presentation have been improved?"
- "If you had to do it over again, how would you handle the customer's objection about delivery"?

Suggest a Better Way

If a salesperson is unable or unwilling to recognize performance deficiencies—because of lack of experience or lack of cooperation—suggest a better way to use the skill or knowledge being coached. Similarly, when the salesperson agrees with your critique, don't merely discuss a shortcoming. Be prepared to provide better options and be sure to expand on them.

Elicit Feedback

After discussing what needs to be done to improve or maintain performance, ask for feedback to make sure the salesperson knows what you expect him to do. Don't settle for short answers like, "I got it" or, "I understand." Have the rep repeat in detail what you and she have agreed to, as well as how and when it will fit into a specific sales situation. Also, get some feedback on how he plans to gain or practice the skill, if needed.

Encourage Practice Using the Skill

Even if the salesperson assures you that he perfectly understands and will use the revised skill constantly, remember that you are dealing with a skill. Most skills need live verification verbally, to insure that you are both on the same page. Informal role practice is ideal; you pose questions and challenge the salesperson to respond. Even a full role-play in the car, for example, will give you super feedback as to how she applies your suggestions. Other methods to encourage practice:

- An application assignment that requires the salesperson to study/learn information.
- Use a virtual coaching series to gain ongoing feedback and to monitor and enhance improvements.

Get Commitment

Rather than just tell the person to use the new skill or knowledge that's been acquired, try to get commitment to do what needs to be done:

- Ask for recap and commitment, even a plan when you're not there.
- Cite the success others have had with the solutions you and the salesperson have discussed.
- Get agreement on when and where he will use the acquired skill(s).

As referenced in Chapter 1, I have provided a Toolbox (Chapter 10) of many pertinent tools that can be used in implementing strategies. There you will find a valuable checklist, the Field Sales Coaching Tool, that summarizes the coaching process and enables you to plan and note key activity during the call, as well as identify strengths and areas to improve, including follow-up steps for the salesperson and account.

Field Coaching Checklist

In summary, the field coaching process should be used in relation to your specific coaching objective—the target skills you want to focus on. However, it is often necessary to shift objectives based on what happens during the presentation. Most important, during field trips make sure to validate the skill improvements gained via virtual sales coaching efforts. In many instances, due to the customer's reactions and responses, as well as the unpredictable direction of the sales call, many strengths and weaknesses can surface. Therefore, it is vital to observe many skills, tactics, and strategies for assessment. Table 2.1 should be helpful in sorting out the basic or core selling skills that often need to be coached.

This checklist would also have value for the salesperson when you introduce a new skill or improve a weak one. I have only been addressing coaching "skills" up until this point because it is more challenging than upgrading or improving other issues. While product knowledge, business acumen, tactics, and personal issues are important, most of them are apparent or measurable and therefore simple to correct or improve via coaching or training. Obviously, they are important along with selling skills and need to be addressed when improvement or reinforcement is needed.

Field Coaching Missteps

Field coaching is a powerful method to build skills, reinforce performance, and enhance your own leadership respect. Unfortunately, some sales managers blow this opportunity by:

- *Taking over the actual presentation, sometimes as a "rescue" pretense, often to show off their own sales skills, or simply to win the business.* I'm reminded of a client with a sales manager whose team's sales dropped dramatically as they grew in staff size. Starting with a few sales reps, he did very well, but as he expanded to 4, 6, 8, and eventually 10 salespeople, they plateaued quickly and then the team's sales went dramatically downhill. The problem was that the manager, a super salesman, literally did the selling for his team, but as they grew, his travel time became exhausting. Now, as a sales manager coach, he's reinvented his success by having them take responsibility for selling per se while he coaches them. On joint calls, he observes, rather than jumping in, and then coaches afterward.

Table 2.1   Checklist for 10 Critical Selling Skills

Critical Selling Skills	Selling Skill Objective	Performance Standards
Opener/ Lead-in	Gain customer's attention and set stage for sales call presentation	• Brief, one or two sentences • States reason for call • Contains benefit, agenda • Gains response from customer
Discovery questions	Learn about customer's business needs and priorities, surface opportunities, and information such as →	• Needs, opportunities? • Product usage, potential? • How decisions are made? • Available budget?
Presentation	Provide customer with a product/service presentation related to business needs, translated into key benefits	• Focuses on customer needs • Stresses benefits over features • Organized by priorities • Requires frequent feedback
Reinforcers	Make the presentation more interesting, memorable, and persuasive by using visuals and third-party success stories	• Uses brochures, visuals • Employs data, studies • Tailors aids to customer needs • Features act as reinforcers
Feedback questions	Ask questions periodically to determine customer interest, understanding, how well your offering fits needs	• Open and closed questions • Ask after key point(s) • Tactful, easy to respond • Will clarify, gain agreement
Handle resistance	Effectively handle or offset customer questions, concerns, stalls, and objections	• Partially agree to set stage • Restate resistance to clarify • Respond effectively to issue • Ask for agreement afterward

Table 2.1   (*continued*)

Critical Selling Skills	Selling Skill Objective	Performance Standards
Gain com-mitment	Get customer to take specific, measurable action (hopefully defined in your sales call objective)	• Use trial closes early • Summarize benefits • Ask for commitment • Determine next step(s)
Control	Manage the sales call presentation, keep It on track, implement sales process	• Implement game plan • Manage distractions • Keep customer involved • Follow company sales process
Listening	Display listening ability by capturing all key points, offer feedback to illustrate understanding of information	• Ask clarifying questions • Summarize key points • Give frequent feedback • Take accurate notes
Personal dynamics	Interact with customer in positive manner, share "talk-time," enhance ongoing relationship and trust-building	• Enthusiasm, energy, passion • Be tactfully assertive • Avoid issues of conflict • Maximize personality/ style fit

- *Trying to cover too much after the call, when they should be limiting the conversation to one or two priority performance items.* As mentioned, in my early days as a sales manager, I subtly took notes when observing, and then covered everything from A to Z, giving the salesperson confusion rather than suggestions. Stay focused on one or two priorities at most, either skills you've agreed to focus on or situations that surfaced during his presentation.

- *Assuming that one coaching conversation will hit home, and neglecting to reinforce the new or enhanced sales skills.* Most new behaviors need to be reinforced four to six times for them to stick.

- *Conducting a one-way coaching conference with the sales manager, monopolizing the discussion and failing to encourage feedback.* Not helpful for learning or motivation.

Check Out Field Sales Coaching Tool in Toolbox

To help you field coach more effectively, I have included a vital aid, labeled Field Sales Coaching Tool, which you can find in the Toolbox in Chapter 10. The tool covers all the steps required for a productive coaching sales call, including planning, setting an objective, the coaching process to follow, notes on your coaching observations, and more. Use it for solid coaching success after observing each salesperson's presentation.

Let's move on to field coaching's frequency-of-contact "partner," virtual sales coaching. As you will quickly learn, virtual sales coaching is a structured process, way beyond checking in with salespeople by phone as needed, or a casual follow-up conversation. While the process is similar to field coaching, you'll find that it is challenging to execute, but at the same time, you will appreciate the huge value it adds to more frequent and more effective sales coaching. If you want to be a master coach, and I hope you do, virtual sales coaching is a "must."

VIRTUAL SALES COACHING

As indicated, virtual sales coaching, a state-of-art partner of field coaching, is vital to gain frequency of coaching contact, which, in turn, generates improvements in performance. Since the sales manager can't actually view and/or participate in the virtual sales call, the feedback stage must be accurately set ahead of time prior to facilitating the coaching discussion.

The following rules are essential for virtual sales coaching, which is largely accomplished by phone and email. I'm calling them rules, simply because (1) this is a relatively new process, and (2) if you don't follow the process steps ("rules") nothing will be gained; in fact, virtual sales coaching is a shortcut, so don't try to shortcut the rules.

Virtual Sales Coaching Rules

Done properly, employing these rules will generate significant coaching frequency, require much less time than field coaching trips, and reinforce your actual field visits. Virtual coaching will also provide unlimited freedom in selecting specific accounts (anywhere) to enable coaching afterward.

1. Select priority skill(s) based on field coaching. Prior to virtual sales coaching, the salesperson needs direction on which skill or skills to work on. Ideally, this focus should be limited to one skill, possibly two. Most important, the sales manager and salesperson together determine the focus but only *after* field coaching. Field sales coaching should precede virtual coaching and lead to agreement on which skill(s) should be a priority for ongoing development. During virtual sales coaching, the priority skill gets initial attention, although the entire sales call can be coached based on what surfaces during feedback.

2. Plan virtual sales coaching and cadence. The sales manager and salesperson determine specific sales calls that will be coached, indicating how many will be in the series. To focus, change, and upgrade one skill, it is recommended that six spaced sales calls (to be coached upon completion) are needed to reinforce and sustain skill improvements. One of the advantages of virtual sales coaching is that specific customers or prospects can be targeted ahead of time, since the sales manager's travel time and availability are not considerations. In terms of "space," the selected sales calls should be scheduled at least once per week and preferably twice each week to maintain continuity and focus. Further, the sales representative should be encouraged to "practice" the priority skill(s) on *all presentations*, especially those sales calls during the coaching cycle.

3. Conduct a pre-call review or conference. Similar to field coaching, a pre-call conference or briefing variation is often desirable. Depending on the needs and experience of the sales rep, it may be necessary to conduct an actual pre-call conference, similar to that employed when the manager accompanies the sales rep on a call (covered earlier in this chapter). The best way to provide a pre-call briefing for virtual sales coaching is to have the salesperson email a copy of his sales call planner for a specific call. You can review it quickly and determine if a pre-call review is needed to discuss it, to provide pre-call coaching, or to make changes before the presentation is made. If concerned, schedule a phone call. If not, respond positively so the rep can proceed with the planned sales call.

4. Provide sales call documentation. Virtual sales coaching will not work without detailed, objective documentation. Objectivity is in the eyes of the beholder and accuracy can be reinforced with field coaching checks, and experience, to enhance accurate communication of what happened. The key element is a sales call report/profile, a short worksheet or tool document, *completed immediately after the call*. The sales call should be documented while the actions and responses are fresh in memory and emailed to the sales manager. A simple, uniform tool will capture the key elements of the presentation: skills used, actions, responses, challenges, and so on. Waiting until the end of the day will only generalize the data, create omissions, and overlap the performance with other subsequent sales calls. A completed sample follows at the end of this segment on virtual sales coaching and a tool with instructions can be found in the Chapter 10 Toolbox.

5. Review sales call feedback, plan to amplify. No matter how detailed the postcall document is, it is open to misinterpretation. Unlike "live" field coaching, where both parties witness the presentation and have a spontaneous coaching conference, virtual sales coaching needs to be preceded by a good understanding of what transpired. The manager, after reviewing the postcall tool, should plan to coach: write questions that will amplify what happened, to get the facts, in-depth rationale, and possible coaching suggestions to improve the salesperson's presentation. Obviously, the sales manager's understanding of what transpired will be enhanced throughout the coaching discussion. To a great degree, this mini-planning session is a plus for the sales manager. Compare it to field sales coaching, where you are instantly challenged to conduct a curbstone conference based on what you just observed.

6. Implement virtual sales coaching process. The virtual coaching process is very similar to the traditional and valid field coaching process, with the exception of the initial step, "Amplify, discuss the sales call." While you should have received a document describing the sales call activity, it is important to get the "big picture" and greater detail on what transpired in the salesperson's own words, and maybe fill in some of the specifics that were omitted from the document. This step will answer some missing info and fill in gaps. Equally important, it will enable you to ask additional in-depth questions on what transpired.

This step is the bridge between field coaching (observing the call) and virtual sales coaching (gaining comparable detailed, objective feedback). It is vital to set the stage for the total coaching process. Here is the virtual sales coaching process, similar to field coaching, discussed earlier, but leading in and featuring the critical Amplify step:

- Amplify, discuss the sales call to gain the complete picture and minute details of what transpired.
- Reinforce positive behavior and skill use, so improvements are sustained.
- Have salesperson analyze the call and surface details to measure his knowledge.
- Use leading questions when necessary to highlight skill gaps or gains.
- Suggest a better way after discussing a weak application, skill, or action.
- Elicit feedback to ensure 100% communication accuracy.
- Encourage practice in using the skill(s) to maintain momentum.
- Ask for commitment to underline importance and follow-up.

Together, these process elements enable the sales manager and salesperson to discuss feedback, ask questions, and move forward with coaching. When finished, the sales manager and rep continue the coaching series and ultimately return to periodic field sales coaching. It's important to complete a virtual sales coaching series of at least six sales calls to gain acceptance/reinforcement of the targeted skill(s). The actual sales skill improvements and salesperson's objectivity (in providing feedback) can best be validated by field coaching follow-up to observe skill gains, and, of course, sales performance results.

Virtual Sales Coaching Cadence

Virtual sales coaching requires a cadence, which is critical for both the individual's reinforcement and continuity of the enhanced sales coaching campaign. Ideally, the virtual sales coaching campaign should have this recommended cadence to maintain what I call the 3 Rs: Rhythm, Reinforcement, and Retention.

- First, a field coaching visit to observe skills and "live" performance. Do basic coaching, hopefully on multiple account calls, and discuss skills, performance with salesperson to determine and agree on coaching priorities.

- Virtual sales call coaching series should include six postcall conferences, ideally after two scheduled sales calls per week, for three weeks; communicating the need for practice on all sales calls is a vital part of virtual sales coaching.
- Depending on results, added options may be to:
  - Continue virtual sales coaching on similar cadence, adding another campaign or cycle, focusing on same or other needed skill(s).
  - Complete virtual sales coaching series and assume that the salesperson will sustain improvements.
  - Follow up via field coaching to determine if improvements are realistic, and/or to validate salesperson's feedback objectivity and accuracy.
  - Set up a revolving schedule with sales team, working in sequence with each representative for three weeks to do virtual sales coaching for specific skills, or simply to help the sales team sustain performance at the desired level.

Virtual sales coaching will obviously increase the sales manager's coaching frequency with unlimited number of contacts potential. However, to maintain cadence as indicated above, to allocate the proper coaching for designated reps, it is recommended that no more than two cycles (two different reps) be conducted simultaneously. This will spread out the coaching to about one session per day and provide adequate focus and scheduling, while optimizing each coaching session.

Based on experience with virtual sales coaching, it is estimated that the typical coaching session will take about 30–45 minutes. This is more than field coaching, which often takes 5–10 minutes, right after the call. The added time and discussion are needed for briefing and questions, to bring the sales manager up to date, and, of course, for coaching. If done right, there will be no interruptions or pressure to "run to the next call."

See the following feedback tool that salespeople can use to brief you, written immediately after the sales call presentation. It should set the stage for a meaningful discussion, coaching recommendations, and to connect the communication going forward.

Most experts agree that sales coaching per se is the #1 priority for every sales manager with a team to direct and develop. Unfortunately, as indicated earlier, field coaching, while ideal, is limited due to other activities, travel time/cost, and available field time, along with difficulty in coordinating schedules. That's where virtual sales coaching will help you "hit a home run" if you follow the "rules" and practice it so your priority is accomplished in top fashion. I doubt if you will find another source for virtual sales coaching, the other half of the dynamic duo, so study the guidelines and practice it to achieve ongoing coaching success.

As promised earlier, a sample feedback tool (salesperson's document of sale call) follows. You can find a blank tool in the Toolbox in Chapter 10, as well.

Virtual Coaching Tool, Postcall Analysis for:

Alice Mayweather

Account: *Zone Supreme Co.*   **Date of sales call**: *01/03/00*
Decision-maker: *Albert Jones, PA*   **Priority skill(s):** *Complete sales process*

Sales Call Analysis	Responses
My sales call objective: *Complete planned sales call and get commitment for Super Product order*	Achieved: Yes No Comments: *Partially achieved, finished call and tried to close but he wants to talk with boss.*
If not, why not?	*Jones is not the real decision-maker.*
How well did I execute my priority skill(s)?	*I think I did a good job although failed to close.*
What was the most effective element of my sales presentation?	*Selling benefits of Super Product.*
What could I have done differently or better on this sales call?	*Qualified Jones as decision-maker when I made the appointment.*
What did I learn that I can use on other sales calls with this account?	*Always make sure that decision-maker is involved.*
My biggest obstacle in this sales call and what I did to handle it:	*Customer said he did not have application, but I think I found one that he seemed interested in.*
What ideas did I gain that I can use with other accounts?	*Always plan the call with decision-maker in mind.*
Next steps or strategy for this account?	*Follow up with Jones and try to get order or trial. If not, get to decision-maker.*
Other comments:	*Having trouble with pricing and feel awkward discussing it with customers, or when to bring it up.*

Sales Management Success: Optimizing Performance to Build a Powerful Sales Team. Copyright © 2019 by Warren Kurzrock. All rights reserved.

My earliest date and time to meet with you by phone: *January 6, your convenience*

ALLOCATING COACHING FREQUENCY TO MAXIMIZE RESULTS

How you allocate your "coaching visits" (both field and virtual) among your sales team members is one of the most significant actions in your playbook. Allocating coaching frequency where you can get the best payback is a great method to generate improvements and provide an ROI for your time. There are basically three types of coaching frequencies or methods. One is to coach everyone with the same frequency, which I refer to as "routing." Another method is "crisis" to rescue a plateaued or failing salesperson. Neither really works and both methods are anachronisms from another era. The third method, allocating coaching frequency according to need and payback, is ideal.

Now that we have determined how field and virtual sales coaching together can multiply your total coaching frequency, let's look at how frequency gets allocated among team members to increase results. Two important, related questions need to be answered by every sales manager: "Who do you coach, and how often?" The broad rule is "everyone needs coaching," even the superstars. However, to maximize the coaching effort, discrimination is essential. This enables the sales manager to allocate or share the coaching frequency among the team members based on the reps who can provide the best long-term payback: Who has potential for individual performance growth and sales results?

Many sales managers allocate coaching instinctively, but the coaching is often driven toward salespeople who are failing for one reason or another, or because some reps constantly need help in "closing the deal." In my early sales manager days, selling a transactional product (copiers), I was happy to respond to each need. If a salesperson was not producing demos or sales, he or she got immediate attention. On the other hand, salespeople, who felt the "boss" on a joint sales call would help in making the sale, constantly yelled for help. I soon learned that both types of support were not effective or even a good use of my time. In short, coaching needs to be allocated effectively to improve overall team performance and maximize sales results.

Allocate Coaching Based on Need and "Coachability"

As stated, everyone needs coaching, but the ideal way to balance your overall coaching effort (both field and virtual sales coaching) is to allocate "visits" for each salesperson based on two individual, related factors: (1) potential/need to improve skill-knowledge and (2) "coachability" willingness to absorb your coaching and practice it on a continuous basis.

For example, why spend extensive coaching time with a salesperson who needs to improve but is reluctant to adopt new skills, ideas, and practice when you are not there? In a perfect world, both of these characteristics need to be assessed for each salesperson so they can be integrated to determine who gets the most coaching, who gets moderate coaching, and who gets minimum coaching. That's what sales coaching allocation is all about, with the ultimate benefits of improving the sales team's performance, and spending your time to get the best return on your investment of coaching time.

The ABCs of Coaching Allocation

To implement this segment of the strategy, identify the salespeople with room/desire to grow, and who are coachable, and coach them most frequently. Salespeople who are low on potential for growth—those who are at a top level already, or ones who have shown little or no improvement over time, even if coachable, should get less coaching time. The overall objective is to break your sales team into three groups: A, B, and C, based on coaching allocation. The As will get the most coaching, the Bs will be coached less (about half the frequency of the A group), and finally, the C group will be coached on a low frequency, since there is little to gain from frequent coaching. I hope this makes sense, since it's based on the Pareto law of the "important few" and "unimportant many," validated in different versions by countless successful sales managers. To summarize before I get into the "how to":

- The As have potential/room to grow skills and knowledge and are coachable.
- The Bs have some growth potential and are coachable.
- The Cs have little or no growth potential, and may or may not be coachable.

Salespeople who have good "potential/need for skill-knowledge improvement" are the best candidates for your coaching efforts, assuming they are coachable. These salespeople are neither the most nor the least knowledgeable or skilled, but they have the most room to grow. In some instances, they are relatively new salespeople, or eager ones who seem to be stuck at a moderate level. If they are coachable, good coaching and more frequency can change these salespeople from average to very good performers.

A salesperson with good skill-knowledge improvement potential, who is also coachable, will often provide you with a good return on your investment of coaching time. On the other hand, someone with low skill-knowledge potential would probably not provide a good return on your investment of coaching time, even if coachable. A lot of time can be wasted trying to turn the least knowledgeable or skilled salespeople into "good" producers. Usually working to "save" them in the field doesn't vastly improve the situation. Retraining, counseling, or discipline may be better solutions for the weak producer or the one with a low potential level of skills or knowledge.

The second dimension sales managers need to analyze in determining how much time (frequency, that is) to spend coaching a salesperson is coachability. Coachability means how easy and effective is it to work with the salesperson? Is she receptive to your ideas? Does he want to improve? Is he enthusiastic about the job? Does she willingly apply your recommendations and continue to practice between coaching sessions? Do you see improvements, even small ones, after coaching? All these elements are part of the factor we call coachability. Salespeople who are highly coachable—those who are receptive to ideas and have the basic ability to do the job—are most likely to provide a positive return on the sales manager's investment of coaching time.

Ranking Individual Skill-Knowledge and Coachability

How do you assess (1) skill-knowledge and (2) coachability? You can use your gut instincts and judgment to sort the team into A, B, and C groups or employ a short version of Porter Henry's proprietary Skill-Knowledge and Coachability assessments to accomplish a workable plan. Simply rank your salespeople on both issues using 75 points (our measure) to assess both needs. Here's how.

For both skill-knowledge and coachability, rank each salesperson with the appropriate point spread:

High: 50–75 points

Medium: 25–50 points

Low: Less than 25 points

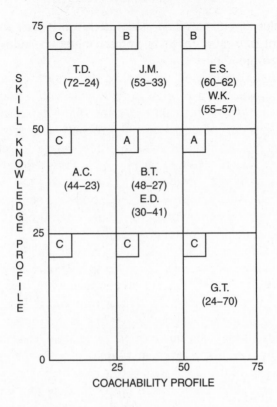

Figure 2.1   Field Coaching ROI Grid

For example, a typical salesperson, Barbara Thompson, who has good skills and knowledge with some room to grow might be ranked at 48, and along with reasonable or medium coachability, could be given a 27. The two interacting scores together when charted help provide a guide for coaching frequency as illustrated on the Field Coaching ROI Grid chart in Figure 2.1. The A, B, and C categories define which group each person falls into.

As you can see, Barbara Thompson (BT), based on scoring above, is an A candidate on the chart. The interacting scores in parenthesis, when charted, indicate who should get the most/least coaching time and enable you to profile your sales team into A, B, and C groups for coaching allocation:

- "A" salespeople, with room to improve and who are coachable, get the most frequent coaching based on your judgment (what is needed to make improvements).

- "B" salespeople, who have less need to develop, yet are coachable, get moderate coaching frequency, about half as frequent as the A group.
- "C" salespeople, with few development needs, receive coaching on low-frequency basis, roughly one-fourth as often as the A group.

While many coaches instinctively assess a person's development needs, few consider coachability. With heightened coaching frequency, coachability ranking becomes more important in sorting out where you can get the best payback for your coaching time and capability. This process, initially complicated, becomes routine with use. The key is to recognize the two values, determine them with some accuracy, and apply them in your coaching allocation efforts.

Planning Sales Team Coaching Frequency

As stated, in a typical salesforce allocation, the A salespeople (including new recruits) will determine the ideal or maximum coaching frequency, the B group will be coached about half as often, and the C reps, about one-fourth of the A group frequency. For example, if the A salespeople are targeted for monthly coaching, B reps will be coached every other month, and the C group will get coached every fourth month. With experience coaching your sales team, you will be able to determine the best frequency for the A group and then use that to select appropriate frequencies for Bs and Cs.

Obviously, your coaching planning should include both field and virtual sales coaching, giving you more flexibility, reach, and necessary frequency. Keep in mind that in a typical field coaching day (most industries), you can build in four to six coaching calls. As you will learn, true virtual sales coaching takes about a half-hour per session and needs to be done in a series (about six spaced coaching calls) to generate the proper frequency and reinforcement. A useful assumption, comparing a coaching day with six virtual sessions, is that virtual sales coaching requires about half the time needed for field visits. This data should help you in planning and optimizing the sales team coaching allocation for individual development and to achieve/sustain the sales team's peak performance.

Here's an example of a Quarterly Sales Coaching Plan used by a sales manager to both plan and make sure that his target of 30 days coaching is met. This schedule reflects both field and virtual sales coaching plans.

Sample Quarterly Coaching Plan

Total visits/campaigns planned for sales coaching during quarter: **30**
Salesperson allocation priority:

Priority	# of People	x	Frequency	x	Duration	=	Totals
A	2	x	8	x	day/cycle	=	16
B	3	x	4	x	day/cycle	=	12
C	3	x	2	x	day/cycle	=	6
					Total days allocated		**34**

In the above example, the sales manager has allocated more time than originally budgeted or planned for. In order to meet this quarterly plan, the sales manager has a number of options. He can increase planned coaching to 34 or cut back on allocated days to 30 by reducing frequencies. Another option would be to downgrade one of the sales-people, such as moving a B (a marginal or "low" B) to a C. And of course, the sales manager can also increase the virtual sales coaching campaigns (cycles) to replace a few of the field days. Let's face it, a virtual campaign of six virtual coaching sessions will certainly take less time (three to four hours) than a full day of field coaching.

Sales Coaching Strategy Review

Now that your planning is done, let's close the coaching chapter with a few reminders.

While the actual coaching is fun and challenging, allocating coaching among the sales team is a "must" if you want to benefit significantly. Keep in mind that your relationship with each member of the sales team is a true partnership that enables every salesperson to share or determine her goals, assess strengths and development needs, which you ultimately agree on. Mutual sharing in this partnership will accomplish significantly more than one-way coaching from the sales manager.

The bottom line is that you need to be analytical in assessing coaching needs and behaviors, transparent in offering constant feedback on devel-opment needs and successes, and democratic in accepting/negotiating the salesperson's ideas. And don't forget to properly reinforce skill gains so they are sustained.

Implement the sales coaching strategy this way with each team member:

1. Create preliminary A, B, C categories for salespeople based on experience (adjust yearly), determining individual groups based on charting skill-knowledge needs and coachability.
2. Start the strategy with field coaching visit(s) and agree on individual strengths and one or two skill improvement needs.
3. Employ a series of six calls (minimum) for virtual coaching focused on one skill.
4. Implement other series later, possibly now (if not satisfied with feedback), or schedule on A, B, C coaching allocation.
5. Field coach with rep as needed to validate and reinforce gains, and set the stage for future virtual sales coaching.

While you may not follow this strategy in detail as laid out, implementing the major concepts in your own style or format will surely improve your coaching and your sales team's performance. Above all, make sure you capitalize on the dynamic duo, field and virtual sale coaching. Go for it.

3

A Strategy for Managing Sales Performance

YOU HAVE PROBABLY HEARD a version of the comment: "Sandy is a great salesperson because she _____"

- knows how to sell value.
- is fantastic at prospecting.
- sells strategically at high account levels.
- has super closing skills.
- has an awesome personality.

The true fact is that few salespeople succeed by performing *one* skill, activity, or behavior well. While the superstars may have a dominant skill or behavior, they usually exceed expectations because they have mastered a variety of the critical sales skills, tactics, and strategies and can build them into a winning combination.

Considering that there are a multitude of skills, behaviors, strategies, and actions that make up the "complete salesperson," how does the sales manager know which buttons to push and what actions to take for development purposes?

MANAGE PERFORMANCE GAPS BEFORE THEY BECOME PROBLEMS

Our research in studying and observing thousands of salespeople on the job has validated that most salespeople have a need/capability to perform (rotate, repeat) about 50 actions (skills, subskills, behaviors, decisions) during a typical selling week. The bottom line is that the typical sales manager manages 10 people (on average) but also needs to track and monitor their 500 combined skills and behaviors being used differently on an ongoing basis. Equally important, he has to constantly monitor that the right ones are being used, that they are employed in the right sequence, and make upgrades and changes when needed. It's an awesome task for any sales manager without a strategy or system for highlighting the problems early on and hopefully taking the right action.

A great sales trainer (now an independent consultant), Will Voelkel, who I've had the pleasure of working with for many years, described the problem this way:

> One of the greatest challenges a sales manager faces—besides exceeding quota consistently—is that rare ability to determine the most appropriate action to take when there is a performance problem with a sales rep. As a corporate sales trainer with a global company and as an independent consultant to hundreds of clients, I frequently witnessed the challenge in action. Too often, sales managers have their own "go to" solutions: retrain the salesperson, coach them, team them up with a star performer, or—the worst possible scenario—ignore the problem and hope it will go away by itself.

Aside from new salespeople, most sales managers rely on revenue (increase, decline, or flat) to determine who needs help the most, and if they can find time, they try to pinpoint a deficiency and go to the rescue (often too late, focusing on the wrong problem). In today's economy, the situation is compounded by the plethora of demands on the sales manager and the priority struggle to supervise 8–12 salespeople with varying needs, problems, and limited time to allocate to managing per se.

What every sales manager needs is a "crystal ball"—a simple system (with minimum time investment) to organize and monitor activity, predict where the problems will occur, and then focus on the right solution at the right time. To manage sales performance effectively and efficiently, a sales performance system is desperately needed. If you are not convinced, take a minute to consider the benefits of learning and utilizing a strategy that this chapter will unveil.

Benefits of a Managing Sales Performance Strategy

Aside from efficiency and effectiveness, a strategic approach and process provides many benefits for sales managers, in particular:

- Recognize performance "warning signs and symptoms" before they become sales performance problems.
- Analyze a wide range of performance indicators that many managers overlook.
- Proactively develop their people by identifying gains and gaps in expected performance.
- Determine the root cause of a performance problem, which often points to the best solution.
- Select the most appropriate actions to reinforce gains and eliminate gaps.
- Follow an efficient system to drive sales performance and results.

Overview of the Managing Sales Performance (MSP) System

Let's begin the process by offering a detailed model that enables the sales manager to seamlessly strategize and manage the sales performance process on an individual salesperson basis. There are four critical steps in the sales performance model that are used for analyzing performance:

1. Communicate/ Monitor Critical Success Factors	2. Identify Performance Indicators (Gains/Gaps)	3. Determine Causes	4. Take Appropriate Actions

Each step can best be understood by reviewing the "big picture" of the model shown in Figure 3.1. A detailed explanation of each step will then follow.

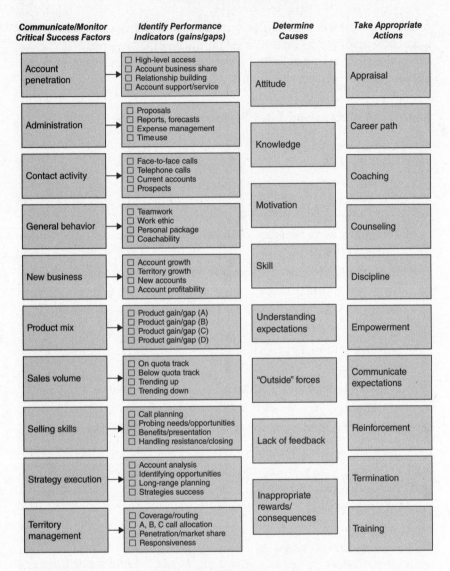

Communicate/Monitor Critical Success Factors	Identify Performance Indicators (gains/gaps)	Determine Causes	Take Appropriate Actions
Account penetration	☐ High-level access ☐ Account business share ☐ Relationship building ☐ Account support/service	Attitude	Appraisal
Administration	☐ Proposals ☐ Reports, forecasts ☐ Expense management ☐ Time use	Knowledge	Career path
Contact activity	☐ Face-to-face calls ☐ Telephone calls ☐ Current accounts ☐ Prospects		Coaching
General behavior	☐ Teamwork ☐ Work ethic ☐ Personal package ☐ Coachability	Motivation	Counseling
New business	☐ Account growth ☐ Territory growth ☐ New accounts ☐ Account profitability	Skill	Discipline
Product mix	☐ Product gain/gap (A) ☐ Product gain/gap (B) ☐ Product gain/gap (C) ☐ Product gain/gap (D)	Understanding expectations	Empowerment
Sales volume	☐ On quota track ☐ Below quota track ☐ Trending up ☐ Trending down	"Outside" forces	Communicate expectations
Selling skills	☐ Call planning ☐ Probing needs/opportunities ☐ Benefits/presentation ☐ Handling resistance/closing	Lack of feedback	Reinforcement
Strategy execution	☐ Account analysis ☐ Identifying opportunities ☐ Long-range planning ☐ Strategies success	Inappropriate rewards/ consequences	Termination
Territory management	☐ Coverage/routing ☐ A, B, C call allocation ☐ Penetration/market share ☐ Responsiveness		Training

Figure 3.1   Sales Performance System

MANAGING SALES PERFORMANCE STRATEGY AND MODEL

The expanded model in Figure 3.1 may look a little terrifying at first glance, but I guarantee if you read this chapter carefully, you will quickly learn how simple and effective it is. And when you opt to use it with your sales team, you will cherish the benefits and results it generates. Here's a description of the key elements and concepts.

Column 1: Communicate/Monitor Critical Success Factors

The first challenge is to simplify the sales manager's job by identifying the most critical sales factors, so she can target what's important and not "get lost in the weeds." As indicated earlier, the problem is that the typical salesperson performs so many actions during a typical period (such as a quarter) that they are impossible to recognize, monitor, or change without consistent tracking. Coaching helps but under today's pressure, typical coaching visits miss the majority of sales calls.

For example, as an analogy, consider watching and coaching a tennis player with dozens of skills and actions involved. They include forehand strokes, serves, overheads, backhand, net play, and so on. Each stroke has its own set of subskills: keeping the elbow in, watching the ball, grooving the stroke, adding a top-spin, and so on. What's needed to create improvement is an effective way to isolate (identify) a major deficiency, and then break it down into small steps for practice. The same guidelines apply to sales performance, which is much more complicated and difficult to observe or track than a tennis match.

That's why we have simplified the Critical Success Factors into a manageable 10 categories or buckets, covering the most critical performance issues that create success. While they all interact to a degree, identifying the top 10 enables the sales manager to start with a level playing field and focus on the priority factors, which ultimately define total performance. Once the major categories are defined (there can be more or less than 10 and the Critical Success Factors may differ slightly from company to company), it's essential to communicate expectations for each. Determining expectations for each category sets the stage for the salesperson and indicates "how high he/she is expected to jump."

Communicating expectations for each salesperson's performance is a starting point of good management. Expectations need to be specific and achievable, with complete understanding and buy-in from each salesperson. It's a starting point that can't be omitted or casually committed. If not done properly, it will come back to haunt you later as an "excuse for poor performance" or a lack of understanding the expectations. If you opt for the 10 Critical Success Factors (more or less), set a short, measurable expectation for each one and when finished explaining them to individual sales team members, provide each one in writing. Specific expectations will provide accountability and measurement, along with motivation to achieve.

The 10 interacting Critical Success Factors range from account penetration to territory management. All can be monitored and measured, to a certain degree.

Each of the Critical Success Factors is further defined by the Performance Indicators (next step), which provide key performance measures for each. However, let's go down the list with a "big picture" definition:

1. *Account penetration:* Ability to expand account's business by selling at "higher" levels, building relationships, finding new applications

2. *Administration:* Quality of reports and forecasts, submitted on time; attendance

3. *Contact activity:* Quantity of phone and sales calls, both for prospecting and with accounts

4. *General behavior:* Team player, courteous to support and service staff, building relationships, trust with accounts, work ethic

5. *New business:* Primarily new accounts gained, but also account growth

6. *Product mix:* Achieving targets for different products based on % allocation

7. *Sales volume:* Numbers provided by company, but often distributed late; may not be broken down; good idea to collect your own estimated data/rep so you have it when you do analysis of trends, comparison with quotas

8. *Selling skills:* Gained mostly from coaching, reports, feedback, focusing on 8–10 most important skills, and feedback from each salesperson on his or her perceived development needs and your expectations

9. *Strategy execution:* Implementing company strategy, using generic strategies, long-range planning, identifying opportunities and pursuing them

10. *Territory management:* Allocating frequency of calls based on account importance or potential, territory coverage, and market share.

In summary, you should focus systematically on the top 10 sales skills, some of which are more important than others, as opposed to randomly examining a myriad of subskills that can drive good or weak performance. For the sales manager, the first step requires (1) setting/communicating expectations for each category and (2) observing and tracking performance (collecting data, critical events, on-the-job observations, interactions with salespeople). While company data is generated on revenue, the balance must often be identified from reports, coaching, and observation.

Column 2: Identify Performance Indicators (Gains/Gaps)

In tracking activity for one of the 10 categories (Critical Success Factors) that impact sales performance, the manager notices a shortfall or change in a performance indicator. This should trigger a move to getting a more defined or finite fix on the issue, thus identifying the performance gap. The system provides an inventory of four Performance Indicators for each Critical Success Factor. Obviously, there could be more than four indicators, or some that are more important in your business, than the ones we have included.

For example, Critical Success Factor for "Selling Skills" identifies four important skills as gains or gaps to review, which you should be familiar with:

1. Call planning
2. Probing for needs/opportunities
3. Benefits/presentation
4. Handling resistance/closing

There are certainly more than four selling skills, but these are four top ones in core selling performance, often where the gap (or gain) is hiding. When assessing a potential problem or gap in a Critical Success Factor, be prepared to dig deeper than the four gains/gaps we've provided. The four in each case are major symptoms or possibilities, but don't hesitate to look further or go deeper even if it requires a preliminary discussion with the salesperson involved.

Let's examine another set of Gaps and Gains from the Critical Success Factor (model). Consider Account Penetration as an example.

As sales manager, one of your salespeople has plateaued and his sales from existing accounts has started to taper. Based on this and supporting reports and coaching trips, you suspect he's not building or penetrating his current accounts even though there is potential. Seeking clues, you move to the next, adjacent column, Identify Performance Indicators, to find one or more gaps that are fueling the performance slowdown. Based again on your observation, notes, reports, or clues, you then pursue one or more of the following (taken from the model), questioning the possibilities:

- *High-level access* (Is he calling high enough, possibly reaching C-level?)
- *Account business share* (In major accounts, is he beating the competition's share?)
- *Relationship building* (Seeking, building new relationships and contacts?)
- *Account support/service* (Is he providing enough support and service?)

The ultimate conclusion or problem may be one of these, or all, or even a different account penetration gap acting as the culprit. However, the MSP model offers four clues to start the self-questioning process to lead you, as sales manager, to the gap or problem. This is a simple analytical problem; step 2 is defining it and moving toward the best solution.

Once the gap(s) is identified, you can make an informed judgment: Is this a serious gap (i.e., pipeline prospects have dropped 50%), or should I just continue to monitor it? As part of the analysis (for each sales team member), the sales manager has to monitor other Critical Success Factors to see if there are other gaps, since all 10 interact together to drive overall performance. *They are often related and impact one another.* For example, a gap in "Contact Activity" will impact other Critical Success Factors. Assuming the gap is serious, or there are multiple gaps in other Critical Success Factors, you can move to the next step with confidence.

Don't forget reinforcement! Up until this point, I have largely focused on gaps. Let me put in a reminder about gains, which are also important. Gains can be made at the expense of gaps, so a gain could also be a red flag. More often, it is a value or improvement to be recognized by the sales manager and reinforced so the salesperson continues it as part of his or her performance menu.

Column 3: Determine Causes

The rationale for finding causes is logical. The cause can often determine the solution and point to the appropriate sales manager action (or possibly multiple actions). In a perfect world, it takes the guesswork out of your solution selection. In a less than perfect situation, it will help you determine the best of 10 actions to take (as shown on the chart).

As you can see on the MSP Model chart, there are eight possible causes. Here they are with my comments adjacent (in parenthesis). It should be apparent that this is a guide, and there is no magic solution for every gap or performance problem. The ultimate cause may also overlap with another and actually consist of two interacting challenges, such as a salesperson with a poor attitude who is demotivated because she is not getting enough feedback (or attention) from the manager. Having said that, here are the eight causes as a basic guide and my brief comments:

1. *Attitude.* If you feel that a sales rep has an attitude problem affecting performance, counseling, discussed in Chapter 4, is probably a good place to start.

2. *Knowledge.* Lack of product, application, account, or industry knowledge requires added training.

3. *Motivation.* Counseling as a first step may help you confirm that motivation is the problem, which is always difficult, and then determine why the salesperson is demotivated, and possibly enable the right action/solution. Handling motivation is a huge challenge, yet it is extremely important. That's why it is covered in detail in Chapter 7.

4. *Skill.* Coaching is the perfect solution for skill improvement; if it doesn't work, counseling may be needed to find out why.

5. *Understanding expectations.* It should be obvious that either you or the sales rep missed the proper communication—that is, time to review and cement expectations in her mind.

6. *"Outside" forces*. This means that the marketplace may be slow, depressed, or a weak economy is probably affecting most of the team members. No easy formula for this cause. Just recognize it, share with the team, seek positive results and their input going forward.

7. *Lack of feedback*. Smart sales managers provide frequent performance feedback, both good and bad, since most salespeople want it. If you have been remiss with an individual, it may come back to "haunt you."

8. *Inappropriate rewards/consequences*. Rewards should be easy to make in terms of recognition or career direction, but don't be short on consequences when needed. See more on this in Chapter 4, along with some thoughts about discipline and even termination.

For example, if a sales associate has a skill problem, such as handling objections, the logical and perhaps obvious solution is coaching. But if the same gap or skill deficiency is lack of confidence or aggressiveness, it may be an attitude or motivation issue and require a different solution. There are no easy answers to every deficiency, but if the cause can be determined it will often point to an appropriate action (or combined actions) that you can take to help alleviate the problem and ideally foster a turnaround. As you will see in the following section, most of the 10 sales manager actions can also be used for positive reinforcement in addition to bridging a serious performance gap.

Column 4: Take Appropriate Actions

The final step in the ongoing process is acting on the solution. Many sales managers fall back and assume "one solution fits all" to problems, but they need to have a full menu of solutions and be skilled in their use and application. The model provides 10 viable solutions, many of which are positive to offer reinforcement or to create improvement. They range from Appraisal (can improve minor performance gaps) to Training (when knowledge or skills reinforcement are called for), but a full complement must certainly include coaching, counseling, communicating expectations, use of discipline, and so on.

This book covers most of the 10 solutions in different chapters, and active sales managers should be familiar with some of the infrequently used applications because you never know when a specific action is needed to improve someone's performance.

I'm reminded about a managing experience with a salesperson named George, who I inherited when I received my first big promotion to Regional Sales Manager. George was older than myself, a senior rep, who had excellent performance. However, his sales began to taper and it became apparent that he was unhappy at being "passed over" for a new manager (me) from a different region. During a few informal counseling sessions, he finally indicated that he was bitter and had the right performance and skills to be a manager.

While our company was not big, although expanding rapidly, we had no formal growth ladder. However, I promised him that if he could rebuild his territory and sustain his good performance, I would create a ladder for him to develop and support his climb up. He performed well and within a year the company approved my recommendation for three field sales managers (each selling and managing a small sales team) and George became one of them. A few years later, when I resigned to start my own sales consulting/training practice, George got my job hands-down. Happy ending in this situation. Counseling was the proper action to take, and George was smart enough to eventually share his motivation and ambition so we could find a reasonable and effective solution. Attitude was certainly the cause.

Here's a quick review of the 10 viable sales manager actions, including definitions and when each one works best:

1. *Appraisal*

    Most organizations have a yearly appraisal process that enables the manager to review the total performance of the salesperson. If yours does not, I recommend you read up on it and implement it with a generic form (you both fill out on the rep's performance list and compare viewpoints). Without getting into the details of implementation, it is a great action to generate feedback, look at the person's overall performance, learn about her goals, and improve some of the little things that may bother you (or the sales rep!). Since it is usually done annually, don't wait for the appraisal to deal with a major performance problem. Overall, it is a great opportunity to step back and comfortably review performance from both sides.

2. *Career Development*

Many salespeople are interested in moving beyond their current position at some point and are motivated by future opportunity. While not everyone is motivated or has the potential to move ahead, you can certainly encourage the right people to prepare themselves and most important, maintain their sales performance at the same time. Don't overdo it, or use it as a tool with the wrong people. At one point in my career, I had a boss who promised everyone he recruited and hired that they could be a manager someday. And while we were a growth company with many potential jobs, few made it to manager status and many were frustrated by his promises, which literally triggered our sales turnover (including his termination eventually!).

3. *Coaching*

Hopefully you have read Chapter 2 on field and virtual sales coaching, or the Dynamic Duo. There's nothing more important in skill development and sales rep motivation, gaining market knowledge, and building relationships with your sales team than coaching per se. If you are new, get on the coaching bandwagon quickly and master the coaching skills discussed in the previous chapter. It should be #1 on every sales manager's development hit list.

4. *Counseling*

Counseling, unlike coaching, is the best solution for dealing with motivation, attitude, or bad behavior problems. Don't confuse it with a "private conversation" since counseling is a valuable but serious skill. You will learn more about when and how to employ it in Chapter 4.

5. *Discipline*

Discipline is not something you will use often with the sales team, but it can be useful for minor, consistent problems like turning in reports late, not putting enough time into forecasts, or for conflicts with a team member or support person. I've covered some suggestions for this in the Chapter 4, particularly when counseling doesn't work.

6. *Empowerment*

Many of today's salespeople are motivated by empowerment, as you will learn in Chapter 7, which focuses on motivation strategy. In brief, empowerment dovetails with two of the priority motivations, *autonomy* (operating individually on your own) and *mastery* (the desire to learn more, acquire skills, be at your best). Empowerment, given to the right salesperson, can be a powerful motivation and development tool.

7. *Expectations*

Expectations, as covered earlier, are critical for performance measurement. Make sure they are specific, communicated effectively (and often!), with realistic challenges. When someone's performance falls short, it's time to review the expectations to make sure they are understood. It's also critical to raise the bar when appropriate.

8. *Reinforcement*

Driving sales managers, intent on improving performance, often forget to reinforce skill improvements or fail to do it the right way. Without the proper reinforcement—specific, timely, frequent—as covered in Chapter 2, coaching only provides half the potential benefits to you and the coachable salesperson.

9. *Termination*

The ultimate solution for a performance problem that can't be corrected is, of course, termination or firing. When and how to terminate are important, covered in the counseling Chapter 4, obviously when other methods (or the salesperson) fail to correct a major performance problem.

10. *Training*

When knowledge (sometimes skill deficiency) is the cause of a performance shortfall, training is needed. This can trigger re-training, a formal or online course, or simply a review. The important thing is to recognize when training per se is the best solution and to make sure it happens in the right way.

IMPLEMENTING THE MANAGING SALES PERFORMANCE STRATEGY

This strategy is proven and will work with minor customization for any salesforce. However, it requires added tools for monitoring, capturing data, and tracking performance of each individual. This is not an easy job unless you have the discipline to collect the data, analyze performance, and implement changes that are needed.

Effective implementation requires the ability to employ the data and to document critical performance events for each salesperson on an ongoing basis. I recommend a *quarterly review*, which may take a few hours to check and analyze data/notes for the average-size sales team, followed by an accompanying plan for individualized action (accomplished during the next quarter). It should be apparent that major gaps or a serious event should be addressed immediately, rather than waiting until the quarterly review. With a simple spreadsheet planner, the sales manager can review the entire team's individual performances at the end of the quarter, and develop an action plan for specific salespeople who require reinforcement or need to upgrade performance in identified areas. I've provided a sample tracking and action device, the Sales Performance Tool, that capitalizes on the model to track individual performance and your actions, when needed, on a quarterly basis. The sample tool follows at the end of this chapter and you will also find detailed instructions and a master copy in the Toolbox in Chapter 10.

Here are a few important concepts to keep in mind. First, this strategy and process or one like it (if it exists) is not an automatic decision-maker, although as indicated, it is a very useful crystal ball for looking ahead and anticipating performance. In simple terms, it is a strategy that will enable you to track and identify performance challenges before they become big problems (often too late to change). It will make you a better manager, which is the bottom line, with a method for predicting potential, individual gaps and taking the best action necessary for improvement. Second, what you see here is a structured model, which may be analytical overkill for certain managers and sales teams. However, by learning the process, and adopting it to your own useful degree, you will gain both knowledge of the process and the discipline to manage more effectively. At the same time, it will enable you to organize the countless sales team activities, and most important, drive results for your sales team.

Forecasting as a Performance Success Factor

Forecasting per se is a critical and broad tool in managing sales performance, particularly if you rely on it in looking ahead. Unfortunately, many sales managers, account managers, and salespeople treat it as a necessary admin task and nothing more, and put it away as soon as completed. While it is important in every type of B2B selling, it is critical in selling to complex accounts and, more important, measuring progress and strategies. On our master chart, you will see it listed under Administration, but recognize that its success overlaps and helps drive all 10 Success Factors. It can also act as a "whistle blower" for individual salesperson gaps. Since it is a little out of my sales and management experience, and most clients have their own confidential forecasting format, I asked a hands-on expert to share his ideas:

> Missed sales forecasts? Many sales forecasts are built on the salesperson's assumptions, not the customer's decision criteria. The forecast is then missed as the salesperson assumptions were not tied to actual metrics from the potential customer (even if the salesperson had a sales strategy plan). One of the main reasons for a missed forecast is that a sales strategy plan likely failed without a way to measure its accuracy. One of the fundamentals of a sales strategy plan is having a strategy that is tied to a qualification checklist to test and retest the sales plan throughout the sales cycle. At minimum, a sales strategy plan for an account should include a qualification checklist to understand the *customer's* timing for purchase, driving need, funding, and an authority level (signature for purchase order/agreement). A qualification checklist should be written at the start of the sales cycle and include driving need(s), funding, authority, competition, sizing, specifications and any other areas that are relevant to the sales cycle. This qualification checklist should then be utilized by the sales team and reviewed on a regular basis with sales management to retest the plan to look for not only what is working but what is *not working* in the plan (or needs refocus). By reviewing and retesting the qualification checklist throughout the sales cycle, the sales strategy will have a higher probability for closing the sale, which will result in a more reliable forecast!

Thank you, Mike. Michael Kurzrock is currently a veteran sales/sales management leader in the software security industry (yes, my son!).

Applying MSP Strategy with Your Sales Team

As indicated, I have included a completed sample of a two-page, foldout tool with the action pages at the end of this chapter. The Toolbox version includes the MSP Model as page 39 for a reminder of the MSP process. The sample is filled in to illustrate the sales manager's perceptions, data, and actions that will ultimately be taken to help the salesperson do more prospecting. Feel free to use this tool as a model with your sales team to track each person's performance, and then review individually on a quarterly basis. You will find a blank copy with instructions in the Toolbox in Chapter 10.

Regardless of whether you adopt Porter Henry's Managing Sales Performance System, a proven strategy, or invent your own crystal ball, remember these seven critical steps and issues when using this strategy to manage sales performance.

1. Set challenging expectations and communicate them effectively as a foundation.
2. Determine the critical success factors for your business (no more than 10) or match them with ours.
3. Track gains and gaps for critical success factors; take immediate action if serious or repeated extensively.
4. Prior to "instant" or quarterly action, try to determine the cause, which may point to the best solution.
5. Review your data quarterly and share with each salesperson.
6. Take appropriate action, if needed, to improve performance.
7. Use every opportunity to specifically reinforce gains when they occur.

These steps are crucial for managing sales performance in a winning format. This is a very important strategy and implementing it mentally, shooting from the hip, is destined for failure. Sales managers desperately need a strategy with documentation and steps like the ones listed above to make it work. Use Porter Henry's model or your own, along with a tracking plan similar to the three-page foldout that follows. It's a badly needed super strategy that you can customize to your needs and that of your sales team.

With experience, you will find that this strategy is essential for managing individual sales performance, growing your sales team, and above all, creating sales results. It is the ideal foundation for success. The sample Sales Performance Tool follows.

SALES PERFORMANCE TOOL: John Adams, Q2

Success Factors	Expectations	Gains/Gaps	Facts/Metrics	Possible Cause(s)	Manager Actions	Results/Next Steps
Account penetration	Grow each active account by 10% annually	Seems to be on track				
Administration	Weekly reports on time, forecast could use a little more work					
Contact activity	Make 10 prospecting calls per month	Call reports indicate not doing enough prospecting	Checked call reports and determined five prospect calls per month pace for quarter	Doesn't like to prospect, apparently not motivated to do it.	John must do more prospecting. Spend time on coaching prospecting calls SOON.	If coaching doesn't work on improving prospecting, set up counseling date for serious discussion.
General behavior	Follow company policies					
New business	One new account monthly	Sold one new account during quarter	New account was referred by account in another territory	Obvious lack of prospecting has cut new account acquisition seriously. He understands my expectations.	Mentioned to John on 6/15. He claims doesn't have enough time for prospecting.	Gap is getting bigger.
Product mix	Current mix is 20% sales for each of five current products	Okay on mix				
Sales volume	Increase volume 5% per quarter	Volume for quarter is flat	Did $200,000 against, quota $210,000			
Selling skills	Master all skills with current focus on basic skills, and negotiating	Did excellent job on selling skills during my two coaching visits				
Strategy execution	Execute strategy to sell to Fortune 1000 accounts					
Territory management	A accounts seen weekly, B accounts monthly, C accounts each quarter	Routing okay				

4

Counseling Strategy for Attitude and Performance Problems

MOST SALES MANAGERS DON'T understand the difference between sales counseling and sales coaching, and admittedly, they do overlap. Yet there is a huge dichotomy in terms of need, execution, frequency, and impact of these strategies.

Let me underline the difference and overlap with a real-life example. Back in my frontline sales manager days, I had a salesperson, named Chuck, who had most of the skills to become an effective salesman. He had performed reasonably well initially, but his sales numbers flattened out after six months. With coaching, it was easy to determine the cause. Chuck could not follow a game plan and often talked too much about non-business topics, taking him further away from the sales track. As a result, his personality and charm stood out, but his selling skills were in a parking position, forgotten most of the time during presentations.

After three separate coaching days with Chuck, including informal role practice with me, there was little change in how he organized or delivered a presentation and he was defensive and resistant. Coaching had failed to upgrade his performance or results, so I decided to schedule a counseling session with him.

During the one-hour counseling session, Chuck admitted he was stubborn, and had always sold his way—with personality and a loose organization; he firmly believed that you could not structure a sales presentation. However, now recognizing this as a serious problem, he agreed to work hard and change, and we put together a three-month plan that would enable him to practice/demo his improvements on the job. During this action-plan period, Chuck got added coaching from one of my supervisors and their feedback indicated some change, albeit small improvements.

After three months, I joined him for some coaching and ideally to observe positive changes. On his first complete call, he demonstrated better control and organization, although his presentation was far short of perfection. In spite of his shortcomings, he made the equipment sale! When we talked skills afterward, he was not defensive (as previous) and eliminated the usual excuses. Long term, Chuck eventually rose above the plateau he was on and became a reasonably good salesperson. Counseling was the right decision because it changed his stubborn attitude and focused him on eliminating bad habits and improving selling performance. Coaching alone could not accomplish this.

I've been involved in and observed many counseling situations with client sales managers where counseling per se helped the performance-needy salesperson to change attitude, behavior, and even motivation to move ahead to success. When done the right way, it opens the door to solutions and improvements.

COUNSELING DEFINED

Since almost everyone is familiar with coaching per se, let's compare it with counseling to underline the differences. As you read earlier, sales coaching is an ongoing "must" for salesperson development and skill improvement, although under today's time and travel limitations, actual field coaching is being done less frequently (virtual sales coaching to the rescue!). Too often it is implemented on a "wing and a prayer" when a problem surfaces and a salesperson needs an emergency visit. Even when performed effectively, sales coaching has its limitations, since it can't solve every performance challenge. That's when counseling comes into play as a valuable alternative skill.

Counseling, as often defined, is focused on solving individual sales performance problems usually caused by poor behavior, attitude or motivation. Coaching is based largely on improving selling skills, while counseling helps solve problems caused by attitude or when coaching fails to create change or improvement.

First, let's compare the two sales manager skills and their application as they work together but are implemented separately with individual salespeople as needed. Take a look at Table 4.1.

Coaching is often easier to execute since the sales manager is primarily dealing with defined, observable skills and tactics. Counseling, to the contrary, is more challenging since it deals with motivation, behavior, and attitude—all intangible, personal causes that usually create observable performance problems. After the counseling need is determined and validated in the mind of the sales manager, then he or she should act. At this point, a whole set of counseling skills must be in place. In essence, counseling is correcting a problem or situation that you (and possibly the salesperson) may not know the cause. The counseling session may also be marked with surprise denial and defensiveness by the salesperson, especially when the goal, expected change, or purpose surfaces.

Table 4.1   Comparison of Sales Coaching with Sales Counseling

Criteria	Sales coaching	Sales counseling
Used best for:	Skill development	Behavior/attitude change
Where accomplished:	In the field, or virtual	In private setting
Techniques:	Observe, coach skills, or get documented feedback from rep after the call (virtual coaching)	Search for, agree on problem, use counseling to determine solution, plan
Objective:	Gradual skill improvement	Short-term turnaround or elimination of problem
How accomplished:	Coaching process requiring time and reinforcement	Finding causes and getting solution plan implemented
Follow-up:	Ongoing coaching visits, virtual sales coaching	Successful action plan completion, reinforcement

---

DETERMINING WHEN COUNSELING IS NEEDED

There are a number of issues, mostly reoccurring, that can and should be resolved with counseling. Counseling has huge sales-improvement value and can be used most effectively in situations like these:

- *When coaching fails to work due to resistance or reluctance to change.* There are many salespeople who outwardly agree with their sales manager's suggestions but do nothing after she departs. Other salespeople overtly resist change. Then there are reps who are creatures of their own selling know-how and habits, and prefer to stick to what they do. If these types of salespeople are not meeting sales or quota expectations, then counseling is needed to create change.

- *Resolving negative issues like work ethic, not following policy, plateaued performance, poor attitude, conflict with others, and so on.* Every sales team member can have problems like the afore-mentioned, and particularly when they are reoccurring for a salesperson, counseling becomes the tool of choice.

- *Motivating turnaround performance often prior to last-options of discipline or termination.* In every salesforce there are sales reps who are failing or headed for failure, often for no apparent reason. The indicators may be a drop-off or slump in sales performance, or lack of improvement over time. Many sales managers resort to heavy coaching, warnings, discipline, and may eventually determine that termination is the best move. If coaching doesn't work, counseling may be needed to surface the problem or solution, prior to termination. Even if the cause doesn't surface, an action plan determined during counseling may awaken a new attitude as the last chance to succeed.

- *Setting the stage for long-term career development.* The prior three situations are problem-solving categories for counseling, and career development should not be overlooked as a positive counseling process. Both are similar, but since problem counseling is much more challenging, I'll focus on that. However, keep in mind that positive counseling is a great way to give recognition and reinforce performance. It is also a method for you to learn about each salesperson's ambitions, personal life, motivations, and to build relationships along with trust.

At one time, I was working with a client who insisted on showing a short video at the beginning of my workshop series on sales management. It featured a well-known consultant/college professor discussing his Significant Emotional Event (SEE) theory, which to me parallels counseling to some degree. To make his point, the professor tells the story of a hippie-type student who parked his bike in the classroom repeatedly in spite of requests and warnings by the professor. After being totally ignored for a few weeks, the professor carried a baseball bat into the classroom and in front of the class, destroyed the bike. His final summary remark on video tape, as I recall, was: "Guess what? He never brought a bike to class after that, because the Significant Emotional Event got his attention and created change."

To some degree, much less than the professor's action, counseling a problem is a Significant Emotional Event for the salesperson. It is designed to get instant, undivided attention and hopefully create positive change. When the sales manager calls you for a private meeting, you know it is serious, with the SEE stress underlying the importance of the situation. Effective sales managers should recognize specific situations that demand counseling, when to counsel rather than coach, and to avoid "shooting from the hip" decisions. This is not easy and determining when counsel may be needed is as challenging as how to deliver the counseling session.

Knowing when to counsel is important, but so is knowing when *not* to counsel. When serious behavior indicators are validated, they should be reported to human resources. Serious problems like alcoholism, drugs, gambling, or illegal activities, and financial or personal problems should not be handled by the sales manager by design under any circumstances. If not HR, recommend professional counseling.

At one point, one of my better reps had his sales take a serious downtown during a good quarter for the rest of the sales team. I decided to counsel him on his performance to find out what was causing his decline since he performed effectively during recent coaching visits. I'm not sure if it was the counseling session or my persistence in discussing options for improving sales, but he finally admitted that he had some personal problems and was spending less time in the territory. The counseling session ended with no plan for improvement, just a commitment on his part triggered by my expectation that he had to manage his personal problems and improve sales. I suspect counseling subtly made him recognize the threat to his job and I learned later that he joined AA to eliminate a drinking problem. Over time, he became more engaged with good performance, and spent many productive years with us in sales.

There is no magic formula for identifying indicators of a problem that needs counseling rather than some other solution. The effective sales manager must be able to identify and validate indicators, pinpointing them with evidence, before starting. This takes thinking and analysis since every organization has its principles and each sales team is unique.

PLANNING TO COUNSEL

Once you identify a problem that can best be modified or solved with counseling, you should follow the following essential steps in implementing the planning phase of the strategy.

1. Pinpoint Observable Indicators

It is critical to begin the counseling solution with a clear-cut description, documented if possible, of what the problem is, how it is impacting performance of the individual or sales team, and how frequent it has happened. It's dangerous to counsel without a full description (and data) to validate the problem and its ramifications.

2. Identify Possible Causes

While the sales manager can seldom determine the cause in advance, she needs to brainstorm possible causes to be prepared for the counseling session. For example, is the cause:

- Not working hard enough?
- Lacking confidence to be aggressive?
- Insufficient motivation, complacency?
- Outside interests taking too much time?
- Strong ego, stubborn?
- Doesn't understand expectations?
- Comfortable with plateaued performance?
- Coaching is not working to improve skills or presentation?

The better prepared with anticipated causes, the more effective you will be in surfacing the real reason. Once accomplished (ideally, documented!), and agreed-upon, the solution will be easier to implement.

3. Prepare the Opening

How the findings are presented is a matter of integrity and tact. This is no time for "dancing" and an effective opening will set the stage for a productive counseling session. It should be brief and cover the indicators as perceived. Ideally, the opening should be brief but cover the following:

- State specific behaviors and results.
- Review related performance expectations.
- Review positive past performance.
- State purpose of session, emphasizing performance improvement.

For example, a realistic and productive opening might sound like this:

"As you know, Sam, your sales are off 10% in the last two quarters, and it seems to me that your prospecting effort, one of your previous strengths, has fallen off. My objective today is to verify what is causing this sales drop and to plan how you can use the second half of the year for a strong finish."

4. Prepare and Plan Questions

The key to conducting a counseling session is surfacing causes and this can only be accomplished with planned, targeted, and leading questions. Continuing with the previous example, some critical, important questions might be planned:

"Do you know how much prospecting you have done during this period?"

"What do you think is causing this drop-off in performance?"

"Are you aware that your prospecting time has dropped about 50%?"

"Are you capitalizing on social media?" "How do you use it?"

"How do you implement your prospecting and how much time do you spend on it?"

"Is there anything else that might contribute to this fall off?"

5. Schedule the Session

You need to pick a private location (office, hotel, conference room) and allow adequate time to conduct the counseling face-to-face. The counseling is an important, confidential session, not something that can be handled quickly or over the telephone, and certainly not conducted in the office where everyone is aware of what's going on and interruptions are bound to happen.

CONDUCTING THE COUNSELING SESSION

Here are some important tips for conducting the sales counseling session:

- *Open the session*. Use the prepared opening to set the stage for the meeting, offering details and documentation to make the case.
- *Wait for a response*. Hopefully, the salesperson will agree or slightly modify your perceptions. In any event, prepared questions should be used to highlight or uncover the causes. Causes need to be stressed and surfaced, since without an agreed-upon cause, a solution will be hard to come by. For example, a sales rep admits to complacency and agrees he is not working as hard as he did initially due to a new baby that has deprived him of sleep. Once determined, the ultimate solution becomes visible and can be part of a plan.
- *Seek solutions*. While the sales manager may know the ideal solution, the chances of it being implemented successfully will be directly related to the sales rep's input. Hopefully, she will contribute suggestions on a solution that includes both participants' ideas and can be finalized in a plan. A detailed plan is critical for success and should include specific actions by the salesperson (and possibly by the sales manager), dates for accomplishment, and how success (performance improvement) will be measured. A timeline for completion is a "must." Keep in mind that for a quick turnaround, or observed change, 30–90 days is the ideal framework for the plan. *Always put the plan in writing*.
- *Gain commitment on solutions*. The more commitment the better.
- *Establish follow-up*. The sales manager must plan to be involved (if not actively participating) in terms of follow-up conversations and feedback to monitor progress. A complete plan is a "must" to insure results.

- *Close session on a positive note.* It's essential for the sales manager to indicate her positive expectations for success and confidence in the salesperson's ability to execute the plan as agreed.
- *Document the session.* In a perfect world, the action plan for improvement should be written together, but if not, complete documentation is necessary to "protect the innocent" against future incidents or next steps, as well as legal protection for the company and everyone involved.

The Toolbox in Chapter 10 contains two tools for counseling, which are vital for executing the counseling strategy and process. The Counseling Planning Tool covers all of the steps discussed so you can plan this initial session. This tool will help you review the steps and this is important for this strategy since you may only employ it a few times each year (ideally). With limited, but important use, you need a guide. If you and the sales rep agree on a solution, you must detail it in writing. That's when the Sales Performance Action Plan becomes essential for success. It enables you both to create a detailed plan that you can monitor to assess success or next steps.

HANDLING RESISTANCE AND AVOIDING MISTAKES

You should also be prepared for pushback from the salesperson since you are challenging his or her performance or behavior. Table 4.2 lists possible defensive tactics that might be encountered along with possible ways to offset them. You may have your own ideas, of course.

Watch Out for These Pitfalls!

There are some common errors sales managers make that interfere with effective counseling.

Don't:
- *Allow too little time for a counseling session.* If you rush through such a session, you won't have time to listen to everything there is to say. The salesperson will feel you aren't really interested and will walk away resentful.

Table 4.2   Offsetting Resistance to Counseling

Salesperson defensive tactics	How to overcome/preempt
Total (insincere) agreement. The salesperson agrees with whatever you say. You sense the agreement or commitment to change is insincere.	If this continues, at some point you must confront the issue directly by saying something like: "You've agreed before yet failed to continue. Why is this situation different and how can we guarantee change?"
Counterattack. The salesperson tries to turn the situation around by placing the blame on you or the company. For instance, he may say, "You don't single out other people when they do this. This isn't fair."	This may be the time to pull your rank and indicate that he is the one being accused or blamed, not you. "As sales manager, it is my right to judge other's performance when shortfalls occur, and that's why you and I are meeting today."
Not my fault. The salesperson claims that other people or circumstances are the cause of the behavioral problem. (Examples: weak market, products aren't selling, my accounts are different, etc.)	Listen and try to understand why it is not her fault, and assuming the salesperson can't support that, continue with your case.
Everybody does it. When confronted with evidence of a behavioral problem, the salesperson claims that "everyone else does it."	Simply indicate that you are not meeting to discuss anyone else, and if others are doing it, they will be called on to change as well.
It's personal. The sales rep refuses to discuss the problem or causes because the issues are too private or personal.	This is a tough one, and while you can insist on sharing the problem, with or without success, possibly suggest he speak with HR or a professional. In any case, you must make it clear that this problem is his or hers to solve and will not be tolerated. Then move on to expectations and plan.
Side-tracking. The salesperson tries to cloud the issue at hand by getting you off the subject, usually by bringing up another entirely different issue.	Basic management is required to demand he stays on subject.

- *Use counseling as a punitive intervention.* This is not the time to "beat up" anyone, so don't go on and on about how awful the behavior is or how you're suffering because of it. Counseling, like all management actions, works best when you protect the self-esteem, confidence, and motivation of the sales rep.

- *Think you know it all.* Don't go in with what you have decided is the "real" problem and the "one-and-only best" solution and spend all your time talking about what you know. It's not your problem behavior and it's not your solution that's the issue. This session is not about you!

- *Conduct counseling with a negative belief about the outcome.* If you believe that, "He'll never change," or that, "This will be a waste of time," your self-fulfilling prophecy will come true. Also, if you really believe that, why aren't you choosing a different management strategy or tactic to resolve the issue?

- *Do counseling in an environment with distractions.* Anything that interferes with the privacy or continuity of the session sends a message that this activity is not all that important—a message that undermines the effort you are making.

What Next?

Hopefully, the action plan will succeed, but if not, the sales manager has options, which depend on HR policy, and the degree of success achieved by counseling. Obviously, the next action depends on changes in performance, which can range from none to improvement, or to a major turnaround in behavior/performance:

- With progress, establish a second counseling session to improve the plan and subsequent objectives and performance.

- With no progress, it may be time to provide discipline. This is generally used when counseling has not succeeded and a severe behavior/performance problem continues. Discipline is proper and fair yet designed to improve performance and is usually a precursor to termination.

- Termination may be desirable at this point. There is also a defined process for providing discipline, which is not covered here because in all cases, the sales manager should consult with management or human resources.

In the final analysis, counseling is a very effective method for creating turnaround in behavior and performance in a relative short time. However, because of the complexity of "when and how" to use it, the sensitivity involved, and the infrequent use for most sales managers, reviewing this chapter's content for implementing the counseling process beforehand is essential for success. As indicated earlier, to help you, please use the counseling tools in the Chapter 10 Toolbox.

Remember to use this counseling strategy for motivation, behavior, and attitude shortfalls, where it works best to determine causes and resolve problems. Dealing with motivation alone is a huge challenge with no easy or obvious answers. In Chapter 7, the complexity and dynamics of motivation are covered, including strategic solutions to align, reinforce, enhance, or even awaken a salesperson's dormant motivation. You will gain a better understanding of today's different motivations and methods to help identify an individual's "drivers." This will also help you connect an individual's motivation to counseling solutions and overall sales performance.

5

Optimize Time to Achieve Priorities Strategy

WHEN A SALES MANAGER fails to achieve (or exceed) his goals and priorities, the blame is often placed on "doesn't coach enough," "did a poor job of hiring," "neglected her sales team," or "focused on the wrong issues." No one ever mentions time as the culprit, since most sales managers work very hard and probably invest more job time than the average non-sales manager. Yet the underlying, ubiquitous, and invisible problem is time and how it is managed. Time is slippery and tough to discipline, yet in most cases of either success or failure, it is the tricky, hidden force that greatly influences final results.

The truly successful sales managers instinctively and in a smart fashion allocate time to optimize payoff and diminish the time-wasters. Unfortunately, no sales manager is born with this instinct and few develop it on their own in their academic growth or prior work assignments. There's little training available in managing time or how to allocate it to accomplish the sales manager's priorities. Yet, time management is one of the most critical strategies you need to manage both effectively and efficiently. Optimizing time strategy can multiply your sales manager impact and efficiency.

THE CHALLENGE AND SOLUTION

As mentioned earlier, and if you are a sitting sales manager, your time allocation world is often ruled by interruptions from salespeople, customers, bosses, emergency travel, and pet interests like email and enjoyable activities like coaching or personal selling. If you have been in the job for a while, you surely recognize that time management and related performance, together, are a huge challenge for today's sales managers. Often with 15–20 defined activities such as coaching, supervising, training, hiring, planning, and so on, including a team of different, demanding salespeople to manage, the job has dysfunctional potential. Add in Type A bosses with demands, many interruptions, and a mix of customer problems. Guess what? Time management becomes a never-ending marathon challenge that needs to be corralled.

This chapter is not only about being efficient or using effective techniques to save time. That alone won't improve performance. The real key is indeed saving time being gulped down by unplanned or surprised interruptions and normal delays, and more important, reinvesting it to achieve your priorities. Saving time and reallocating where it will improve performance are the keys.

The good news is that there is a solution that takes either individual or group training (the latter will enable sales managers to set priorities, exchange ideas and buy-in to successful applications). Here is an overview of the four solution steps that must be addressed:

1. Determine where your time is now being spent.
2. Rank your priorities.
3. Allocate your time based on top priorities.
4. Use effective time management techniques to stay on track.

Let's address them one at time.

DETAILED STEPS FOR IMPLEMENTING THE STRATEGY

If this strategy and its steps seem more complicated than other strategies so far, you're right. While it involves data, calculations, and self–job analysis, the main reasons it is challenging to implement is that it requires different steps to make it happen. The steps involve a personal time study, determining/ranking your priorities, and reallocating time so your major priorities get sufficient time, and finally, performing your strategy with two interacting goals in mind. The goals are to (1) ensure that your top priorities are receiving the time you committed and (2) manage your daily activities, using efficient techniques while avoiding time-killers.

The benefits and rewards should be obvious to you: more efficiency, improved personal performance, greater accomplishment, better job satisfaction, and significant sales team success. Having said that, let's move on to the four different steps.

Step 1. Determine Where Your Time Is Now Being Spent

Most frontline sales managers have 15–20 activities in their job description ranging from sales calls to coaching to attending meetings, and much more. And while they instinctively try to focus on the high-payback actions or projects, they are often driven by emergencies, demands, and little time required for the important priorities.

This becomes much more believable if you do a simple time study of where your minutes and hours are currently being spent. This has to be a starting point, if only to make you believe (or shock you!) where your time is currently being spent, often unconsciously or out of your control. When you compare the time allocation with your priorities, you will probably be surprised that some of them are being short-changed and not getting enough time to get them done properly. For example, coaching is considered a top priority by most experts and sales managers themselves, yet few can devote enough time to get it done effectively. As mentioned elsewhere in this book, surveys have proven that the average sales manager spends less than 10% of her time coaching. Yet, successful sales managers find a way to make adequate coaching time happen by managing their time!

So the starting point—a "must"—is to do a time study so you quickly learn where your time is being spent. I recommend one week at minimum but prefer a two-week individual time study because the averages play out more realistically. Ideally, pick two typical, separate weeks at different calendar times to get the most realistic results. Using the tool on the next page will make it simple since all you need to do is check off time spent on a specific activity in 30-minute increments. When the study is complete, convert your times to percentages for easy comparison. Your analysis will provide unique, and in most instances, surprising feedback.

Take a look at the worksheet that follows and then continue with instructions for how it is used for this first step and subsequent analysis. You might also check out the list of activities to see if it dovetails with your specific job, and to determine if some should be deleted, and others added.

Sales Manager Time Allocation Tool

Sales Manager Activities	Priority A,B,C	Mon.	Tues.	Wed.	Thur.	Fri.	Total Hours	% of Time	Ideal Time %
Administration: general paper/computer work									
Coaching: in field, phone, online									
Company Meetings: attend live, online									
Counseling: individual sales rep problems									
Forecasting: discussion, analysis, review									
Interviewing/Selection: related to hiring									
Management Reports: internal/external									
Managing Sales Team: supervise, communicate									
Marketing: promotions, related activities									
Personal Development: study, review, research									
Planning: strategy, idea generation, future plans									
Sales Meetings: group sessions, live/telephone									
Proposal Writing: help reps, develop input									
Selling: live or phone, with/without rep									
Telephone/Email: sending or receiving, responding									
Training: directing in office									
Travel: include travel done in work hours only									
Other Key Activities:									
TOTALS	XXXXX							100%	

Instructions for using this worksheet are simple:

1. Review the sales manager activities and edit them as needed to make them relative to your specific sales manager's job. Add other activities that may not be listed.
2. Monitor how time is spent for one or two different weeks (latter preferred). This is necessary to provide realistic and average time allocations based on real-world activities.
3. Check off time in 30-minute "buckets" with reasonable precision for time/activity overlaps and objective adjustments.
4. Total time horizontally for each activity for both weeks and convert to percentages.

When these steps are completed for two weeks as suggested, you will have a reasonable, accurate picture of where time is being spent. In the initial review, it would be a good idea to first ask yourself these questions:

- Are there any activities or priorities that required a greater time allocation?
- What was my biggest time-killer (wasted time)?
- What technique(s) do I find useful for managing time?
- Did I meet my expectations for the week, accomplish my objectives?

This exercise will set the stage for the next steps.

Step 2. Rank Your Priorities

Pareto's Principle, often called the 80/20 law, or "the unimportant many, important few," is a proven method for ranking your priorities. I trust that you are familiar with the 80/20 validated sales version: for example, "80% of your company sales come from 20% of the total clients."

Porter Henry Co. has modified the principle to fit the sales arena, using it for territory and account management, and sales manager priorities, as well. Adapted and validated to the sales manager activities, this indicates that 15% of the activities that the sales manager performs are very important for success, 20% are reasonably important, and 65% are minor, contributing little to his or her productive performance. The Pareto Diagram in Figure 5.1 illustrates the concept visually but also challenges you, the sales manager, to prioritize your activities to determine those that are the most important (top 15%) for achieving performance and the ones

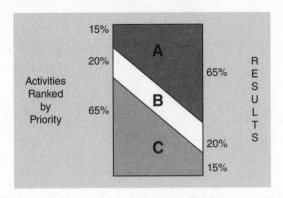

Figure 5.1   Pareto Diagram for Sales Manager Activities

that are next in importance (next 20%), and so on to the leftovers in the 65% bracket.

Having said that, the challenge for you, as a sales manager, is to put time management aside temporarily and identify the A priorities (top 15%) that contribute the most to your success (65%). Assuming 20 activities in total, this means that you need to identify the three (15%) most important activities. For example, depending on the company and job, coaching is often a typical manager's top priority. Yours may be quite different, but it is critical for you to determine the most important priorities and rank them as As. In similar fashion, you have to identify the next important group (20%) of priorities, selected from the activities. These four now become the B priorities, less important for success than the three As. The remaining activities, the less important ones, are labeled C.

The challenge is sitting down and sorting your activities into A, B, and C categories. It's an important decision, and a difficult one, as evidenced in our group training when sales managers from the same company, with similar-size districts and roles, can't always agree on which is an A or B. While you may decide without support from others, it's always a good idea to get a second opinion such as from your boss, another manager, mentor, or friend. When time allocation gets into the equation (shortly), you will see the importance of this decision-making process. The bottom line is allocating enough time to A priorities (not necessarily the *most time*) so they get accomplished effectively, and then moving on to the Bs with the same objective. That's the next step.

Check the sample time study and Priority A, B, C #2 column to see how one sales manager determined his time use and established his priorities:

Sales Manager Time Allocation Tool

Sales Manager Activities	Priority A, B, C	Mon.	Tues.	Wed.	Thur.	Fri.	Total Hours	% of Time	Ideal Time %
Administration: general paper/computer work	C	XXX					1.5	4%	
Coaching: in field, phone, online	A		XXXXXXXXXX		XXXXX		7.5	17%	
Company Meetings: attend live, online	C						0		
Counseling: individual sales rep problems	C						0		
Forecasting: discussion, analysis, review	C						0		
Interviewing/Selection: related to hiring	B			XXXXXX			3	7%	
Management Reports: internal/external	B				XXXXX		2.5	6%	
Managing Sales Team: supervise, communicate	A	XX	XX	XX	XXXX	XXXX	7	17%	
Marketing: promotions, related activities	C	XXXXX				X	3	7%	
Personal Development: study, review, research	C			XX			1	2%	
Planning: strategy, idea generation, future plans	C	XX					1	2%	
Sales Meetings: group sessions, live/telephone	C	XX	XX				2	4%	
Proposal Writing: help reps, develop input	B			XX		XXXX	3	7%	
Selling: live or phone, with/without rep	B	XX					1	2%	
Telephone/Email: sending or receiving, responding	A	XX	XX	XX	XX	XXXX	6	15%	
Training: directing in office	C		X	XXX		X	2.5	6%	
Travel: include travel done in work hours only	C				XXXX		2	4%	
Other Key Activities:									
TOTALS	XXXXX	9	8.5	8.5	10	7	43	100%	100%

Once you have completed steps 1 and 2, doing a time study and determining your A, B, C priority ranking, move to the next step to improve your time allocation.

Step 3: Allocate Your Time Based on Top Priorities

The gold standard for allocating time is to make sure that (1) *the A priorities get enough time to accomplish each one effectively,* and then (2) you apply the same allocation concept for the B priorities. As before, this requires percentage allocation, not hours. *Caution:* As mentioned earlier, *this allocation process does not require that A priorities get the most time allocated, more than B or even C priorities.* The rule is worth repeating again: Start with the A priorities and allocate a percentage of time needed to accomplish each one effectively; then do the same for the B priorities. What's left over then goes to the Cs. This application takes time and thought, but once 100% time is allocated, you will have an ideal long-term target for optimizing time. It can then be converted to hours to create a monthly or quarterly target that can be measured and adjusted, if necessary.

It should be obvious that these target time allocations are just that: "targets." No sales manager can finish a week or month completely on target. However, the time allocations will provide discipline and defense against time-killers, and keep you on the ideal track for priority accomplishment.

Following is the same worksheet, now with the final column on the right completed by the sales manager. As you will see, it contains reallocated times for specific As and Bs updated by the fictional sales manager. Note that some time percentages are increased and others lowered based on his analysis and experience.

The sample worksheet for the final process follows.

As you can see from the completed worksheet, this sales manager reallocated his time percentages for the A priorities as follows:

Coaching: raised time allocation from 17% to 25%

Managing Sales Team: raised time allocation from 17% to 20%

Telephone, Email: reduced time allocation from 15% to 10%

This sales manager also made similar changes for his B priorities, and then achieved 100% by adjusting the many Cs as needed.

Sales Manager Time Allocation Tool

Sales Manager Activities	Priority A, B, C	Mon.	Tues.	Wed.	Thur.	Fri.	Total Hours	% of Time	Ideal Time %
Administration: general paper/computer work	C	XXX					1.5	4%	4%
Coaching: in field, phone, online	A		XXXXXXXXXX		XXXXXX		7.5	17%	25%
Company Meetings: attend live, online	C						0		
Counseling: individual sales rep problems	C						0		
Forecasting: discussion, analysis, review	C						0		
Interviewing/Selection: related to hiring	B			XXXXXX			3	7%	10%
Management Reports: forecasts, performance	B				XXXXX		2.5	6%	3%
Managing Sales Team: supervise, communicate	A	XX	XX	XX	XXXX	XXXX	7	17%	20%
Marketing: promotions, related activities	C	XXXXXX				X	3	7%	4%
Personal Development: study, review, research	C			XX			1	2%	2%
Planning: strategy, idea generation, future plans	C	XX					1	2%	2%
Sales Meetings: group sessions, live/telephone	C	XX	XX				2	4%	4%
Proposal Writing: help reps, develop input	B			XX		XXXX	3	7%	4%
Selling: live or phone, with/without rep	B	XX					1	2%	2%
Telephone/Email: sending or receiving, responding	A	XX	XX	XX	XX	XXXX	6	15%	10%
Training: directing in office	C	XX	X	XXX	X		2.5	6%	6%
Travel: include travel done in work hours only	C				XXXX		2	4%	4%
Other Key Activities:									
TOTALS	XXXXX	9	8.5	8.5	10	7	43	100%	100%

By going through this study and analysis process, you won't accomplish miracles in time management but you will certainly (1) have a solid understanding of where your time is being spent and (2) go away with a realistic, personal set of time allocation targets that will help you accomplish your most important priorities. These two discoveries will enable you to gain a foundation of understanding that will lead to time-management success most sales managers thought was impossible. Start your time study next week!

But that is only the beginning of time management. What's needed to put a red ribbon on the time-management strategy are the best techniques for executing time use and eliminating or sidestepping classic time-wasters that eat into your planning and implementation. That's step 4, which follows.

Step 4: Use Effective Time Management Techniques to Stay on Track

There are many ways to find shortcuts and minimize time-wasters. Following are six useful techniques for optimizing time use that should become habits with adoption, constant practice, and discipline:

Bunch Similar Activities. A useful time-saver to avoid interruptions, "stop and go" activity, and enhance concentration involves doing similar activities at one time. For example, returning phone calls and/or accepting them at one time from 8 to 10 a.m. It enables efficiency and gets more accomplished. This can also be applied effectively when analyzing reports or reviewing/writing proposals and many other similar tasks.

Combine Tasks. Combining tasks, on the other hand, literally means doing two different things at once. It's very useful and efficient when traveling (on an airplane, for example) or waiting for a delayed customer in a lobby. That's why it's always a good idea to carry work-related materials when traveling so you can convert dead time into a productive space. Combining tasks can also be applied efficiently by reading emails and replying immediately at the same time, rather than starting over reading again and writing replies later.

Delegate. You don't need an administrative staff to delegate work to, although if you have an assistant, for example, he will be a good outlet for the tasks you don't enjoy or those that take up too much of your time. However, most sales managers have a great delegation resource that is usually overlooked: *the sales team.* Capitalizing on the sales team is a great way to increase your time availability and equally important, to develop people. For example, you can expand your coaching reach by having your best salespeople coach new or developing sales reps (and develop themselves simultaneously). You can also hand off marketing projects and other tasks to your team, getting work accomplished and building your sales team, while optimizing your own personal time allocation. Delegation like this develops your salespeople and builds teamwork. As you will learn in the chapter on motivation, it can also be a great method to empower salespeople and support their intrinsic motivations.

Establish Routines. Worthwhile routines have a mind of their own and use time efficiently. Some sales managers, for example, have a telephone conference every Monday at a specific time to get sales feedback and to discuss problems. Others set aside time on certain days for call-ins from team members or avoid reading and answering email until the end of the day. Email, while a great tool, is a huge time-waster if not managed. If time for email is not set and maintained, constant checking takes over. Related to email and routines is the concept of answering emails immediately (if deserved) rather than saving them to answer later. Routines are a great way to side-step time-wasters that interrupt other activities and eat up productive time.

Plan Each Day's Activity. The best way to stay on track with priorities and use time efficiently is to have a daily written action plan that prioritizes what you plan to do. Start by listing what you need to accomplish on a specific day, include calendar commitments, and then list activities in order of priority. List the low-priority activities that can be postponed on the bottom. Follow the MIT, or Most Important Task, tactic as well: identify one most important task each day and focus on it until done. The extreme version of this discipline advises you to avoid checking email, taking calls, and so on until the MIT is completed. This MIT technique guarantees that you will get the one important task done every day. Post a sign, banner, or flipchart in your office to remind you of your MIT each day. It's simple but effective time management and a super method to get more accomplished every day.

Set Time Limits. Parkinson's law is a proven adage that says, "Work expands to fill time available until it's completed." A perfect example is a typical phone conference that is set at 30 minutes and often unknowingly goes way over the time limit. This law applies to almost every project or time allocation, including meetings, projects you are working on, writing reports or proposals, long-range planning, and so on. The bottom line is that if you *set a time limit*, you will normally complete the same amount of work or activity in less time. If you fail to set a time limit, the work itself will expand on its own (with you accompanying it and wasting time!).

Time management for sales managers is essential. It is compounded today due to an overload of different tasks and distractions, multiple contacts to deal with (associates, customers, management, sales team), enhanced communication needs, and time-consuming and challenging assignments, all resulting in frequent interruptions and demands. In order to successfully manage priorities, and accomplish more, a priority-time management strategy is vital. The smart sales manager has to constantly battle the invisible, hungry, time-waster monster. Strategy, planning, technique, focus, and discipline are the only keys to success in this arena. Regardless of where you are on the sales manager ladder, you need to manage time as you progress toward greater success. You now have the knowledge and tools for helping you measure and manage time, particularly as it relates to priority accomplishment. Use them to accomplish more than you ever dreamed was possible and help set the stage for your move into the ultimate sales leader ballpark.

Remember to implement the two major issues that really drive this strategy. First, it's essential to check your time allocation yearly with a simple study, as described previously, using your Sales Manager Time Allocation Tool (in Toolbox in Chapter 10 with instructions). When finished, review your current time allocation to ensure that your A and B priorities received enough time to achieve desired results. If not, or if your priority rankings have changed, make positive adjustments in the Ideal Time column for the future. Second, review your techniques to control time-wasters and how they worked to optimize time. If you're not satisfied with overall results, pinpoint the shortfalls in time management and techniques and move forward with your disciplined time management.

6

A Strategy to Improve Team Selling Skills, and Yours!

MANY SALES MANAGERS HAVE come up through the ranks and earned their promotion to sales manager by being a sales star. If that's your case, congratulations on your talent and related abilities that moved you up the ladder.

Even if you have not been a star or were promoted/hired with little sales experience, you should recognize that developing sales skills, along with management abilities, is a never-ending process. You cannot afford to leave your sales skills behind, or let them rust—that is, fail to grow them to a broader and higher level. It's imperative that you learn new, changing techniques and skills, dig in at specific levels, reinforce/improve what you have, and continuously grow your selling skill set.

This warning is not about complacency, but rather, "rust" from nonuse and, perhaps, being overconfident. As a sales manager, you no longer make countless sales calls each week to keep sharp and improve. However, it's critical that you sustain and build skills as part of your sales leader development and momentum. Recognize that selling is your foundation and a critical weapon for sales team success.

Equally important, you have the unique responsibility to train and to instill these skills in each salesperson. Headquarters training does the groundwork, but only the sales manager can reinforce the selling skills on the job and insure they are updated and applied effectively on every sales call.

AN OPEN-ENDED, PERSONAL STRATEGY

Unlike the other strategies in the book, this development strategy for you is open-ended without the usual strategic steps. Simply stated, the goal of building your sales and management skills is too broad, and it defies structure. Awareness is the key, and constantly driving development for your self is the goal. Remember that this personal selling skills strategy overlaps with many of the other strategies in the book, specifically sales coaching, counseling, motivation, and more. However, it's too critical to ignore, so be prepared to invent your own message and steps for self-development. This chapter will underline the skills and provide a tool for you to assess both your current core and advanced skills.

No matter how good or professional your sales approach, ability, and skills are, they will never be totally complete. I've been there and done that. As a salesperson or account manager, you have devoted 100% or more of your focus on selling and probably succeeded by executing skills, tactics, and strategy exceptionally well. Training, instinct, and hard work helped you develop expertise in such skills as "identifying customer needs," "handling resistance," "selling value," "being a strong closer," and much more. This foundation must be retained, of course, but as a sales manager, you need a full menu for your sales team management, because no two salespeople sell exactly the same way, and of course, every customer is different. Most important, necessary selling skills change, driven by products, accounts, competition, and marketing. As the king or queen of selling skills, you are the ultimate consultant for your sales team, their challenges, and their performance.

Once upon a time, as an eager and perhaps "cocky" sales manager, I was training a rookie by demonstrating our approach. Together we called on a large potential account and I made what I thought was a solid presentation, supported with good customer feedback, even to the point where I commented afterward, "We'll do business with this account" and asked: "What do you think?" She quickly replied, "I think we blew the opportunity because he's not the decision maker." She had noticed some subtle comments that I missed, being so involved in presenting, and I had also failed to qualify him. My sales rep was right, and we never got in the door again.

This chapter will do two things to help you determine your track for retention and new learning. First, we'll briefly give an overview of the top 12 sales skill sets that you need to be an expert in. (Of course, this may vary slightly when I check off some of the strategic selling courses, usually advanced, because they may not be appropriate for your business or sales team.) Next, you will be challenged to complete the Porter Henry's Sales *Pro* Performance Indicator. After finishing 60 challenges, you can score yourself and assess your total skill knowledge, while looking at individual skills to identify your own learning needs.

BENEFITS OF BUILDING AND SUSTAINING YOUR SALES SKILLS

At the expense of being redundant, let's look at specifics. As a sales manager, you must own a set of optimal selling skills since they will interact in many phases of the job, as well as enable you to be seen not only as the "boss" but as complete sales leader. Consider these opportunities for capitalizing on your selling skill knowledge and application expertise.

Sales Coaching

On some joint calls, you will have to participate to demonstrate the best way to sell to a specific customer. But on every coaching call, you will have to appraise the full skill set used by the salesperson being observed. Not only will it be important to identify the strengths and weaknesses after the call, but you will have to provide ideas and suggestions for improving the weak ones while reinforcing skills used effectively. This takes knowledge, ability to demonstrate or participate in a sales call, and confidence to make your case when the situation requires it.

Recruiting and Selecting New Salespeople

If your interviewing technique is up to par, the most critical questions you should be asking involve selling skills. Even for candidates with no sales experience, who are motivated to sell, you must determine their ability to absorb, learn, and apply skills with customers, handle rejection, and so on. Beyond questioning and using the right questions, you may also have to evaluate sales performance with advanced techniques like role-play, or even making a joint call with you doing the selling.

You Are the #1 Source for Questions, Advice, and Assessments

During my years in sales, I had a variety of bosses, one very strong on selling skills, others not so good. Guess who I learned the most from? Consider situations in counseling, training, annual reviews, and being a role model. They all mean that you have to stay focused on improving and sustaining your personal sales skill knowledge throughout your career. No one will master the total load, but you need to breathe the content continuously and keep learning. Equally important is your role as a "reinforcer" to power headquarters' training 101 and give constant reinforcement on the job.

Bottom line is that you must attend sales courses and study related product knowledge provided by your company, read sales books and trade magazines, join appropriate organizations and online sales groups, and even take outside courses such as those offered by Porter Henry & Co., Inc., Illumeo.com, American Management Association, Dale Carnegie, or many others public courses. You can also learn from your sales team who individually have acquired useful, effective techniques, possibly different (or better) than yours. Remember, your knowledge of sales skills is the basis for sales leader/sales team success and many sales-related decisions you will make. A strong menu of sales skills and knowledge will earn/sustain your sales team's respect and improve their performance beyond belief.

It will also drive your career, along with sales management development. As a young salesman in my first job selling stainless steel, the only training I received was product and technical training. Quickly realizing the need for selling skills, I took a Dale Carnegie sales course, which helped me get a running start. Months later, I took my brother-in-law, a new salesman in a different company, to a Dales Carnegie open house, but accidently selected the wrong course and wound up in a complimentary speaking/group presentation class. My brother-in-law rejected the course, but I signed up because it offered more confidence and group presentation skills, which I certainly needed. In hindsight, this course dramatically increased my presentation and speaking skills. It also enhanced my career growth as a salesperson, sales manager, trainer, sales executive, and public speaker.

OVERVIEW OF CRITICAL SKILLS YOU NEED TO MASTER AND RETAIN

As mentioned earlier, there are perhaps 50 selling and subselling skills, depending on how the experts sort and name them. Here are the top seven sales skills, from my standpoint and experience, starting with core or basic skills, moving into more advanced, strategic ones. This is a quick review, not an in-depth training course, obviously, so the reader and I are on the same page. As mentioned, you can and should test your skills/knowledge at the end of the chapter for fit and effectiveness.

Consultative Selling

Consultative selling is basically searching for, identifying the business needs of an account, and providing solutions, gaining feedback, overcoming obstacles, and leading to a close. Consultative selling is highly interactive. Depending on the product, account, and type of sale, it can take one sales call or many to gain a commitment. Consultative selling is the foundation for basic, core selling, but also is essential in high-ticket items sold to complex accounts, sometimes called "solution selling." Figure 6.1 depicts Porter Henry's Sales/Purchase Process model, which illustrates our validated consultative selling process. An explanation follows to provide an overview of this successful, interactive process.

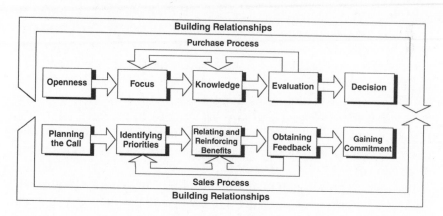

Figure 6.1   The Sales/Purchase Process Model

The model recognizes that selling is *not* a linear step-by-step sales process. The process is unique in that it is totally consultative, based on *how customers make purchase decisions,* a proven defined process that has been validated; the five decision stages are illustrated in the top row of boxes: Once the customer is *Open* to an offering, he/she moves to the *Focus* stage to consider priorities and needs, then collects product and service *Knowledge,* moves to the *Evaluation* stage, and finally makes a *Decision.* During the process, the customer may shift gears and return to a previous stage as illustrated by the arrows above the row of decision stage boxes. You and I go through the same stages instinctively when making a major purchase such as a house.

The salesperson uses the "mirror image" stages (directly below each customer stage) to *lead* the customer through each buying stage, hopefully to a positive decision. The five basic skills are: Planning the Call, Identifying Priorities, Relating and Reinforcing Benefits, Obtaining Feedback, and Gaining Commitment. During the typical consultative selling workshop, the salesperson acquires and practices the five core skills in the bottom boxes (stages), learns how to read what stage the customer is in, and applies added subskills such as: building relationships (trust/listening), differentiating the offering, asking impact questions, handling resistance, negotiating to close, and more.

Territory Management

Territory management is critical to every salesperson's success, but it is much more than who makes the most calls during a week. Looking at it another way, the more *high-potential account calls* a salesperson can make in a day, the more he or she will sell. Sales skills are important, but selling is also a territory–numbers game driven by frequency of contact targeted at high-payoff accounts. Most sales territories are covered by instinct or travel-efficient routing. Both methods leave a lot to be desired. The ideal process is to sort the accounts by potential, A (high), B (medium), C (low), and then visit the As more frequently, the Bs less frequently (about half the time), and the Cs infrequently (even missing them on occasion).

Sorting accounts by potential is challenging. It requires analyzing each account by four interacting criteria to determine the chances of getting the business. The four criteria that need to be ranked are:

1. Access (how many decision-makers, how difficult to connect with them)

2. Proximity to account (the closer the better for frequency)
3. Relationship (obviously, a good relationship is ideal)
4. Competition (strong or weak?)

Together, these four potential assessments add up to a total percent to determine the salesperson's chances of success. This "predictive" percent multiplied by the potential account business for the year will generate what is called the Expected Value (EV) for each account. Once the EVs are determined for all accounts, simply rank them by EV dollars, using the Pareto diagram referenced earlier in this book. The top 15% become the A accounts, seen most frequently, while the next 20% are Bs; the Cs are all the remaining accounts.

While this may sound like a lot of number crunching, it needs to be done by the salesperson only once a year for his territory. Once accomplished, the routing is determined by the A accounts to optimize the frequency, including about half the B accounts in the route, and one-fourth of the Cs. This insures the frequency of contact and maximizes results. Time management is needed to eliminate time-wasters, but this, contrary to most "experts," is less important, and accomplished instinctively by hard-working, disciplined, motivated sales reps trying to stretch the day.

Prospecting for New Business

Traditional prospecting is dead. Very few sales calls can be made without an appointment. Retail stores are the big exception. In my early days as a steel salesman, business-to-business cold-calling was the way to go for most metal shops. Later, selling copiers in New York City, all I had to do was find a tall building and start at the top floor. For suburbs and efficiency sake, we quickly moved to the phone to "sell the appointment." Now, prospecting has become more challenging. As you have no doubt experienced, few executives answer their own phone, administrators or other gatekeepers are mostly gone, and voicemail is universally accepted as the way to go. Worse yet, few executives will not return a messaged call unless they know you.

The good news is that social media and email, along with the phone, are powerful tools. The bad news is that capitalizing on these aids takes research time and skills, as well as a complete understanding of social media (hooray for LinkedIn), referral relationships, and using them in combination with the right cadence. Creating phone and email messages are critical, along with knowing who and when to contact, frequency, and when to stop calling unresponsive decision-makers. Just like the auto replaced the horse and buggy, social media has replaced cold-calling. However, the importance of prospecting has probably grown, and this is why today's sales managers need to stay updated and train/reinforce their sales team's prospecting methods.

Multi-level Selling

Navigating an account, finding the right decision-makers, selling at all levels, wide and deep, including the C-Suite, is a "must" strategy for selling complex businesses. While there are a variety of approaches to this type of strategic selling, there is no uniform set of tactics that work for every account. That's why my initial recommendation is to map the account to identify decision-makers and influencers at all levels. Once accomplished, it's important to rank them, not by title, but by influence as it relates to your products or services. Then the real research begins to find out their personal interests, needs, and business preferences. Finally, draw lines to connect them in terms of reporting relationships, common interests, committees, or departments, so you can use one or another as a springboard for gaining a visit based on a personal introduction or referral.

With much of this information collected and mapped out in writing on a visual map, the navigation begins. Salespeople with this kind of a tool, in preliminary format, can search or reach out to key decision-makers in an organized way. While selling and probing skills are key, the multi-level strategy is the ideal way to approach and sell to any complex account. Obviously, there are red flags, like finding the finance director who controls the budget, and the leader of a specific project. Selling to complex accounts is complex itself, due to many decision-makers and influencers, a variety of decision-making processes, and the popularity of committee decisions in today's market. If you don't have this skill in your back pocket, updated to today's challenges, you need to brush up.

Sales Negotiating

Most salespeople (and sales managers) think they know how to negotiate but few do unless they have had extensive training. Sales negotiation is different than other types of negotiating including personal trading (like buying a car) and professional contract negotiations which are often complicated and lengthy. Many salespeople have not been trained in the right way to negotiate, do it infrequently (not good for success), and will often negotiate on the spot when a situation occurs—wrong move. Sales negotiation needs planning since it can be complicated and critical and often impacts the bottom line. These reasons underline the importance for the sales manager to be an expert so he or she can support the sales team, serve as a coach negotiator, and "cover the salesperson's back" when important deals surface.

According to Joan Capua, manager of learning and development for Taylor and Francis Group, "Negotiating is a tough skill for salespeople to acquire." Joan's negotiating credentials include negotiating training for a prior company resulting in an 8% increase in profitable sales, gained by "protecting" margins. She commented further: "Sales negotiating is the most important skill for some salesforces. It's a very difficult skill to acquire for salespeople because they don't negotiate very often, it's very complicated with different styles and tactics, the salesperson is often emotionally involved with closing, and of course, it impacts the bottom line." This certainly underlines the fact that no matter how much a salesperson knows about negotiating, the sales manager has to be extremely proficient at overseeing most sales team negotiations and coaching the team on handling negotiations.

I hope you agree with these comments, but let me highlight some of the key negotiating issues as a gentle reminder of the complexity of negotiations and the importance of you being the in-house expert. The 10 Commandments of Sales Negotiating is a Porter Henry follow-up reminder after the salespeople have learned the nuts and bolts of negotiating such as tactics, style adjustment, making offers, trading for value, and so on.

---

10 Commandments of Sales Negotiating

1. Plan every negotiation in detail! Planning is the single most important aspect of successful negotiating.
2. Stick to the parameters you preplanned. You can almost always come back later if you need to.
3. Don't forget that the customer negotiator is at the table because he/she has something to gain from the sale and the negotiation.

(continued)

(*continued*)

4. Pre-sell sufficiently in the organization, both vertically and horizontally, to build support at multiple levels.
5. Know the value of what you're selling and the issues you can negotiate, and be prepared to communicate the tangible worth of those issues to the customer. This increases your power by increasing your value.
6. Inventory your "power" before every negotiation. You almost always have more power than you realize!
7. Don't put everything on the table early in the sale or negotiation. Hold back on certain offers and trade-offs until later in the negotiation.
8. Never assume you know what the customer really wants. Probe for interests behind positions and recheck them throughout the negotiation.
9. Unless you are intentionally making a concession (giving something without asking for anything in return) as part of your overall strategy, concede and trade off slowly and in increasingly diminishing increments.
10. Do not assume that certain issues are nonnegotiable just because the customer says they are. Almost everything is negotiable.

Selling Value

Everyone "talks the talk" in selling value but most of the value-sellers mean highlighting the value elements of their offerings and benefits with value verbiage. This is certainly a good technique. But delivering quantified value is more effective and certainly more memorable, and a great way to differentiate your offering and company from the competition.

The truth is that most benefits, services, programs, products, and solutions can be valued in concrete terms, or quantified, that is. Take a simple light-bulb sale for example (gleaned from a real-life national wholesaler we worked with). After training, one salesperson was proposing replacement and backup light bulbs for a customer's warehouse. It was easy to validate that his bulbs lasted on average 100 hours more than brand X. That in itself, although important, was not enough to get him the order for 1,000 bulbs. However, when he and his sales manager converted the extra hours to cost savings, and extrapolated it over five years, the estimated but significant savings (in thousands of dollars) got him the order.

Quantifying is convincing and if your salespeople can't find a way to quantify, you, the sales manager needs to train them. It's a powerful method. In brief, almost every product or service has value and it lies in assessing what we call the five value components or indicators using the acronym *IMPACT*. It stands for *I*nventory, *M*oney, *P*eople, *A*ssets, *C*apability, *T*ime. Some of these value indicators exist in most selling situations, either in the product itself or customer application.

For example, product X equipment offers three benefits: produces more at a faster pace, requires only one operator, and takes up less production space. The smart salesperson can measure savings for all three, add them together, and extrapolate the savings over *x* years for significant estimated savings. Even if not precise in mathematics or estimates, this presentation wins over a value words-only discussion because it is significant and powerful. It also illustrates that the salesperson has done her homework! As indicated, this is a skill you need to have, or better yet be able to train and reinforce with your salespeople.

Group Presentations

Group presentations have become a significant selling tool. Major corporations rely on group decisions, which is a powerful reason for employing presentations as a tactic or strategy to gain access to key decision-makers. Gaining access to the decision-makers is often a challenge, and while many executives will not receive salespeople on a one-to-one basis, they will show up for an "important" group presentation.

The challenges are that many salespeople (even top ones) fear the group setting while others lack the knowledge and skills to deliver an interactive presentation to an audience of two to six (or more!) people. As a result, they avoid generating group presentations themselves unless it is a "finals" pitch requested by the customer. One of my early sales training assignments was with a major candy manufacturer whose account managers were armed with Powerpoints to deliver one-way presentations to buyer groups on monthly deals. Prior to training them on how to improve their presentations, we interviewed buyers to get their opinions on how the presentation impacted them. With buyer feedback like "boring," "no discussion," and "too much repetition," it was easy to recognize the major problem: little or no participation from the client staffers. No one enjoys being talked at every month!

Group selling presentations initially require "reading" the group to determine the roles of the attendees, so the focus can be on the "leader" (not necessarily the highest-ranking attendee, but the one who eagerly supports your mission). "Supporters," "experts," and "doubters" should be pinpointed, as well, so the presenter(s) can direct the conversation. In building participation via planned questions, it's essential to get the leader talking (since her words, commitment, and enhancement are a powerful influence). "Reading the participants" and capitalizing on participation is only one part of planning the group presentation, since it behooves the salesperson to plan focused questions, set objectives, determine roles of the presenter's team, identify the key benefits, get feedback, and hopefully plan to lead the group to a consensus decision. Armed with the right skills, knowledge, visuals, and handouts, confidence comes easily and results are optimized.

Are your selling skills up to par and growing? I challenge you to take the following 60 challenge questions to measure your skills or even those of your sales team members.

SalesPro Performance Indicator (SPI)

SPI is a validated instrument designed to assess selling/strategic skills. Your scoring in this book is self-accomplished so I suggest you use a piece of paper to block out the scoring points in the right-hand column, and unveil it after you make your decision for each challenge. When completed, you will earn a score based on your responses to 60 sales challenges.

SPI offers three mutually acceptable choices for each question or challenge. For each question, select the best response and check it off in the appropriate box. Select the *best option* for each challenge to maximize your total score, and to surface sales performance strengths and gaps. Ideally, SPI should be completed in one sitting and you should strive to finish in 30–60 minutes.

When finished, you can assess your score by its total (250 is baseline average). You can also assess your individual skills as follows on the Scorecard, recognizing that each skill is covered in 5 consecutive questions. As you will see, there are 12 skills covered in this exercise, ranging from basic, consultative selling (encompassing 6 related, interactive skills) to 6 more advanced skills, bringing the total skills covered to 12.

(Note: The first six skills together comprise core selling skills.)

Your SPI Scorecard

Sales skill/strategy	Questions allocated	Points scored
Objective, lead in	1–5 (Maximum 25 points)	
Probing questions	6–10 (Maximum 25 points)	
Presenting benefits	11–15 (Maximum 25 points)	
Reinforcing benefits	16–20 (Maximum 25 points)	
Handling objections	21–25 (Maximum 25 points)	
Gaining commitment	26–30 (Maximum 25 points)	
Territory/time mgt.	31–35 (Maximum 25 points)	
Prospecting	36–40 (Maximum 25 points)	
Multi-level selling	41–45 (Maximum 25 points)	
Sales negotiating	46–50 (Maximum 25 points)	
Selling value	51–55 (Maximum 25 points)	
Group presentations	56–60 (Maximum 25 points)	
TOTAL POINTS		

Your sales challenges	Select best option	Scoring points
1. Regarding sales call planning, which of these options is most accurate?	__A. All sales calls should be planned in writing __B. Most sales calls are instinctive, so planning is seldom needed or effective __C. Every sales call requires some planning and the very important ones should be planned in writing	**A = 3 points** **B = 1 point** **C = 5 points**
2. Which of these specs is the *key* characteristic of an effective sales call objective?	__A. Detailed, specific __B. Describes in general what can be accomplished on this call __C. Requires the customer to take action	**A = 3 points** **B = 1 point** **C = 5 points**

(continued)

Your sales challenges	Select best option	Scoring points
3. What would be the best assessment of this sales call objective? "Make presentation on Wednesday to Jerry Holmes at XYZ on new high-speed Hercules motor."	__A. Good because it is specific __B. Not challenging since it doesn't require the customer to act __C. Effective because it describes what the salesperson needs to plan	**A = 3 points** **B = 5 points** **C = 1 point**
4. What is the main objective of the opener or lead-in (initial statement) in a sales call?	__A. Get the customer's attention focused on your offering __B. Greet the customer, introduce yourself and your company __C. Describe your product or service	**A = 5 points** **B = 3 points** **C = 1 point**
5. Critique this opener by selecting the best option: "Hello Mrs. Adams, my name is Jack Jones from Zero Defects Co. I would like to discuss our new cost-saving service, The Bottom Line Report. Is reducing overhead a concern of yours?"	__A. It was good overall and professional __B. It would be more effective if it included a specific benefit such as: "Our customers average 10% production savings." __C. Jack should not have asked a question, which could trigger a negative answer	**A = 3 points** **B = 5 points** **C = 1 point**
6. Questions are essential to get the customer talking and to learn about his/her needs. When selling, however, the questions should:	__A. Be planned and carefully selected, so it doesn't sound like an interrogation __B. Solicit short answers and facts to keep the customer from talking too much and taking control __C. All be open-ended to get the customer talking	**A = 5 points** **B = 1 point** **C = 3 points**

Your sales challenges	Select best option	Scoring points
7. An open-ended question is one that encourages a long answer from the customer. When does this work best?	__A. To get the customer interacting so you can build a relationship __B. To learn more about the business and his/her attitude/feelings about operations, challenges __C. To have the customer expand on a point or objection he or she has raised	A = 1 point B = 5 points C = 3 points
8. A closed question is one that requires a short answer, like "yes," "no", "200 units per month," or "next week." When can this question be most effectively used in selling to customers?	__A. When you don't understand what he or she is saying __B. To learn more in-depth details of the customer's operations or needs __C. To ask for agreement, get a specific point surfaced or nailed down	A = 1 point B = 5 points C = 3 points
9. It's a good idea to qualify a new prospect or customer and determine if he is the decision-maker. The best question to ask would be:	__A. Are you the decision-maker on this project? __B. Will others be involved in this decision and if so, who are they? __C. How do you plan on making this decision?	A = 3 points B = 5 points C = 1 point
10. Financial information is needed during many sales calls: Does the customer have a budget and how does he plan to purchase? What's the best way to get this information?	__A. Don't worry about this until you are ready to close. __B. Ask: "Our solution will cost about \$10–12,000. Is this in your budget?" __C. Ask: "What is your budgeting process for a project of this scope?"	A = 1 point B = 3 points C = 5 points

(continued)

Your sales challenges	Select best option	Scoring points
11. A benefit is best described as:	__A. A description of how your product or service works __B. Your ability to fulfill the customer's needs __C. What the customer gains from buying	**A** = 1 point **B** = 3 points **C** = 5 points
12. What is the benefit in this statement? "You get a higher profit margin because the promotion prices have been reduced. Also, we will not charge for shipping."	__A. Higher profit margin __B. Reduced promotion prices __C. No charge for shipping	**A** = 5 points **B** = 3 points **C** = 1 point
13. An important part of every sales call is the benefit presentation itself. What is the best method to get your points across?	__A. Stress the key benefits with conviction __B. Present benefits first, then features, and ask questions to get feedback __C. Present features and translate into benefits	**A** = 1 point **B** = 5 points **C** = 3 points
14. Regarding benefits, what is the ideal way to present them?	__A. Relate the benefits to customer priorities, needs __B. Start with the most beneficial ones and present them all until you get some positive feedback __C. Focus on features since the benefits are usually obvious to the customer	**A** = 5 points **B** = 3 points **C** = 1 point
15. How would you rate this benefit presentation statement: "Our just-in-time steel delivery will eliminate downtime. Will that speed up production for you, Charley?"	__A. Good because it has two benefits __B. Good because it relates the benefit(s) to a priority (need) __C. Good because it contains all the characteristics of a benefit statement	**A** = 1 point **B** = 3 points **C** = 5 points

Your sales challenges	Select best option	Scoring points
16. The main reason for using visuals, third-party testimonials, data, brochures, and other sales tools is:	__A. They reinforce your words and make the benefits more tangible, credible, memorable __B. They help hold the customer's interest and enable him to understand __C. They help you organize and remember key points in your sales pitch	A = 5 points B = 3 points C = 1 point
17. The most effective tactic to employ when using a visual:	__A. Hand it to the customer to read or handle, get her involved __B. Read it to the customer, highlighting key points __C. Show it, reinforce your point, ask a question to get feedback	A = 3 points B = 1 point C = 5 points
18. When finished using or showing a visual:	__A. Advise the customer you will give her a copy __B. Put it away so it is not a distraction __C. Leave it in plain view to reinforce the point	A = 3 points B = 5 points C = 1 point
19. When showing a brochure or using another tool, it's a good idea to:	__A. Highlight the key points with a marker or pen __B. Keep it unmarked with a new, clean appearance so it looks professional __C. Have the customer hold the brochure and point to areas you want him to see or read	A = 5 points B = 3 points C = 1 point

(continued)

Your sales challenges	Select best option	Scoring points
20. You plan to show a prospective customer an important, complex Powerpoint presentation on your computer, but she objects by saying "I don't have time for that. Just give me an overview."	__A. Provide a quick overview to meet her request and determine her interest __B. Set up another date indicating that this is too complex to simply verbalize or overview __C. Email the Powerpoint presentation and promise to follow up and answer questions	A = 3 points B = 5 points C = 1 point
21. Select the best option for describing an objection (sales resistance):	__A. It is a request for more information __B. Needs to be handled immediately __C. Can often be anticipated and planned for	A = 3 points B = 1 point C = 5 points
22. What is the best way to respond when a customer raises an objection?	__A. Clarify the objection with questions to make sure you fully understand the customer's concern before responding __B. Get in step by partially agreeing or showing empathy with her concern before answering __C. Respond directly to offset the resistance while it's on the customer's mind	A = 5 points B = 3 points C = 1 point
23. A customer raises the classic objection: "Your price is higher than we are prepared to pay." Once you understand and qualify his concern:	__A. Try to negotiate to a price that is win-win __B. Sell him on the value of your product or proposition __C. Find a less-expensive solution or product, or be prepared to walk away from the deal	A = 1 point B = 5 points C = 3 points

Your sales challenges	Select best option	Scoring points
24. A potential customer indicates that she is satisfied with a competitive supplier. The most effective way to handle this:	__A. Comment about their shortfalls and sell her on your ability to fill the competitor's gap __B. Compliment her on her loyalty and indicate that your goal is to provide backup and become the #2 supplier __C. Acknowledge her comment and continue selling	A = 1 point B = 5 points C = 3 points
25. The customer/prospect says: "It's hard to believe we can get these results."	__A. Show results from other customers __B. Indicate that many prospects initially raised the same question before becoming good customers __C. Ignore this since it is a minor objection or stall	A = 3 points B = 5 points C = 1 point
26. What is a good definition of closing?	__A. Getting the order __B. Completing your presentation as planned __C. Achieving your sales call objective	A = 3 points B = 1 point C = 5 points
27. When is the best time to close (ask for order or gain commitment)?	__A. When you have finished your presentation __B. When customer agrees with major point/benefit __C. At any time, the earlier the better, or when you sense "buying signals"	A = 1 point B = 3 points C = 5 points

(continued)

Your sales challenges	Select best option	Scoring points
28. A good example of a choice close would be to ask:	__A. Have you decided whether it is a "go" or "no go" on the equipment purchase? __B. Do you want the order shipped to the factory or warehouse? __C. Can we go ahead with the order?	**A** = 3 points **B** = 5 points **C** = 1 point
29. You have done a good job of presenting to a new potential customer. She responds with "Looks good. Let me think it over." Your best action at this point:	__A. "I must have left out something. Can we review the presentation so I can alleviate any concerns?" __B. "Why do you have to think it over?" __C. "Good idea. When can I get back to you?"	**A** = 5 points **B** = 3 points **C** = 1 point
30. The key characteristic or requirement for successful closing is:	__A. Good knowledge of closing techniques __B. Frequency of tactful closing attempts __C. A good presentation preceding "the close"	**A** = 1 point **B** = 3 points **C** = 5 points
31. From a productive sales standpoint, the ideal way to cover a territory is:	__A. Visit all the accounts in a geographic area when you are there __B. Allocate calls based on account volume and potential even if it involves more travel __C. Focus on the "hot" accounts at the expense of others	**A** = 1 point **B** = 5 points **C** = 3 points
32. The ideal time to plan your territory coverage itinerary:	__A. The night before __B. Monthly __C. Quarterly	**A** = 1 point **B** = 5 points **C** = 3 points

Your sales challenges	Select best option	Scoring points
33. In visiting accounts, a good practice is to:	__A. Work by appointment and focus on key decision-makers only __B. See as many people as possible since you seldom know which people can influence a decision __C. Visit with people in a buying mode, those who have a project/application or problem	**A** = 1 point **B** = 3 points **C** = 5 points
34. When ranking accounts to determine importance or potential, it's best:	__A. To research sales and volume so you can target accounts by size __B. Not to worry about data since the time investment is not worth it __C. To consider account potential, your share of business, competition, access to decision-makers	**A** = 3 points **B** = 1 point **C** = 5 points
35. Categorizing accounts by existing business and/or potential, such as A, B, C, enables salespeople to:	__A. Spend more time on sales calls when visiting the highest potential accounts (As, for example) __B. Call on the A accounts with more frequency than the Bs and Cs __C. Organize accounts so each zone/group of accounts can be covered on the same day	**A** = 1 point **B** = 5 points **C** = 3 points
36. The objective of a prospecting call is to:	__A. Make a presentation __B. Sell the appointment __C. Qualify the account first and then sell the appointment, if qualified	**A** = 1 point **B** = 3 points **C** = 5 points

(continued)

Your sales challenges	Select best option	Scoring points
37. Prospecting is best accomplished	__A. When regular customer sales activity slows down __B. On an ongoing, planned basis __C. When time permits	**A** = I point **B** = 5 points **C** = 3 points
38. Prospecting works best by:	__A. Using many methods like telephone, email, social media, customer referrals __B. Focusing on the method that works best in your business __C. Employing the one that you are most comfortable with	**A** = 5 points **B** = 3 points **C** = I point
39. You have phoned a high-potential prospect three times and left messages but have not received a return call. Your best action at this time:	__A. Stop wasting time on this prospect and seek more receptive decision-makers __B. Use a different method such as email, or networking __C. Keep calling. Sooner or later, you will make contact	**A** = I point **B** = 5 points **C** = 3 points
40. How would you rate this prospecting telephone call? *"Good afternoon, Mr. Smith. This is Joe Orange from ACME Industrial. I'd like to set an appointment to discuss how our packaging system can improve your division's service and efficiency. Are you available for 15 minutes next Tuesday?"*	__A. Too aggressive and direct __B. Could have used more benefits to get interest __C. Very good, because it is concise, direct, and the objective was to sell the appointment	**A** = I point **B** = 3 points **C** = 5 points

Your sales challenges	Select best option	Scoring points
41. Multi-level selling skills in complex accounts (with many decision-makers) primarily help a salesperson to:	__A. Sell high, wide, and deep into the account __B. Gain access to the C-Suite executives __C. Get past gatekeepers to sell decision-makers	A = 5 points B = 3 points C = 1 point
42. When confronted with a stubborn or protective gatekeeper, the best way to get to the decision-maker is to:	__A. Contact the decision-maker when the gatekeeper is not available __B. Find a reason why you need to "go over his head" __C. Ask her help to make an appointment and support the request with benefits	A = 1 point B = 3 points C = 5 points
43. One of the challenges in multi-level selling is identifying decision-makers. Which of these tactics is most productive?	__A. Build a relationship with someone in the organization who can help you navigate __B. Research Annual Reports, do online searches, use social media __C. Ask your contact(s) for referrals	A = 5 points B = 3 points C = 1 point
44. An effective tactic in strategic selling is setting up an internal "coach." What's the most important help he or she can provide:	__A. Introduce you to key decision-makers __B. Advocate your product/services and reinforce them at meetings __C. Help you with feedback, direction, and account navigation	A = 1 point B = 3 points C = 5 points

(continued)

Your sales challenges	Select best option	Scoring points
45. It's important to plan and analyze a visual/map of complex accounts showing financial and project decision-makers and influencers. The purpose of this is to:	__A. Determine individual reporting and social relationships, influence, and power for navigating __B. Identify the chain of command so you can plan calls and build relationships __C. Insure that you have covered everyone who can influence a specific sales project	**A = 5 points** **B = 3 points** **C = 1 point**
46. Selling value is another strategic approach. It works best when you:	__A. Mention value on every sales call __B. Identify value as one of the customer needs __C. Quantify the potential value for the customer	**A = 1 point** **B = 3 points** **C = 5 points**
47. The value to the customer is best represented by:	__A. The cost of the product __B. Savings generated by the product __C. The discount offered to the customer	**A = 3 points** **B = 5 points** **C = 1 point**
48. The most effective way to present value is to:	__A. Quantify the potential savings and project them over time, such as a year __B. Cite savings that other customers have gained __C. Ask the customer to determine the value based on your presentation	**A = 5 points** **B = 3 points** **C = 1 point**
49. The best way to uncover value is to:	__A. Ask questions about operating problems to determine value __B. Observe operations on sales calls and note inefficiency __C. Use questions and observation, collect data that measures efficiency or reduced costs in time, personnel, speed, etc.	**A = 1 point** **B = 3 points** **C = 5 points**

Your sales challenges	Select best option	Scoring points
50. You've estimated the savings for one customer: 20 hours of labor per week, involving 3 workers at $15 per hour. How should this value be presented?	__A. Verbally since it is only an estimated savings __B. $46,800 __C. $900	**A** = 1 point **B** = 5 points **C** = 3 points
51. The definition of sales negotiating is best stated:	__A. A situation introduced by the customer to gain an advantage __B. A strategy for resolving value differences that arise during the selling process __C. A method to resolve pricing issues	**A** = 1 point **B** = 5 points **C** = 3 points
52. Which of the options should be the most important when negotiating?	__A. Focus on a single issue such as pricing __B. Plan to introduce multiple issues such as price, delivery, terms, etc., to trade __C. Only negotiate multiple issues when you have to make a concession	**A** = 1 point **B** = 5 points **C** = 3 points
53. When making a concession, the best tactic is:	__A. Make the concession first to build relationships __B. Let the customer make the first concession __C. Try to get equal value in return for any concession	**A** = 1 point **B** = 3 points **C** = 5 points
54. The "trial balloon" (also called "what if") negotiating tactic is a method that primarily:	__A. Presents the account with options you may not be able to commit to __B. Protects you from actually making a commitment __C. Tests the account's position and interests, willingness to accept offer	**A** = 1 point **B** = 3 points **C** = 5 points

(continued)

Your sales challenges	Select best option	Scoring points
55. "Trade-off" is a negotiating tactic for giving and taking concessions. You should always:	__A. Be the first to make a major concession __B. Concede (offer concessions) in small increments __C. Be ready to make concessions even if the customer doesn't ask for them	A = 1 point B = 5 points C = 3 points
56. A good method for handling group or committee presentations:	__A. Avoid them, if possible, because they are unpredictable and challenging __B. Recognize them as an opportunity and even set them up yourself when needed __C. Agree to finals presentations only when you have a chance of closing the business	A = 1 point B = 5 points C = 3 points
57. When confronted with a group presentation, it's a good strategy to:	__A. Plan your presentation in detail __B. Try to make individual sales calls on attendees to learn their "positions" __C. Get your boss or "experts" to join your presentation	A = 1 point B = 5 points C = 3 points
58. When planning a group presentation, it's most important to learn:	__A. Which attendees support your proposition or proposal __B. Who are the "doubters" in the group __C. Who is the "leader" (most influential), not necessarily the highest-ranking person	A = 3 points B = 1 point C = 5 points

Your sales challenges	Select best option	Scoring points
59. When presenting to a group or committee, it is best to:	__A. Limit feedback to avoid challenges, resistance, off-track discussions __B. Encourage as much participation as possible with planned questions __C. Announce a Q & A session at the end to answer questions	**A** = 1 point **B** = 5 points **C** = 3 points
60. You are making a presentation to a group when a "doubter" raises a negative question. While you can respond effectively, the best tactic for dealing with it:	__A. Refer the question to a "champion" or "supporter" to answer __B. Answer it yourself, or ask your "expert" to respond since you are the most knowledgeable about your products and company __C. Acknowledge the concern, and commit to providing an answer with supporting data within 24 hours	**A** = 5 points **B** = 3 points **C** = 1 point

Sales Management Success: Optimizing Performance to Build a Powerful Sales Team. Copyright © 2019 by Warren Kurzrock. All rights reserved.

How did you do on measuring your sales skills? Here's a simple way to assess your performance.

If your total score was *over 250 points* (the baseline), you performed well and have a solid grasp of selling skills and how they are applied. In any case, keep working on these skills and add others so you can build and sustain your expert sales manager role. If you scored *under 250*, get to work, and accelerate your selling skill learning and practice, focusing on the skills with the lowest scores.

Focus on sales skills improvement as much as your sales management development. Together, they are a dynamic to drive your success and that of your sales team.

———

A SELF-DEVELOPMENT STRATEGY IS YOURS ALONE

You may be wondering why I call this chapter a "strategy" rather than a review of selling skills. Strategies often take a long time, are loaded with essential tactics or abilities, and have goals, steps, and demand discipline to make them happen. As indicated earlier in this chapter, this strategy is hard to define because the application is so broad, affecting 90% of your activity and that of your sales team. Therefore, between normal memory losses, changes, advancements, and new challenges, sales skills will always lead selling processes at the frontline level. Calling this development a strategy may get your attention more than naming it a "selling skill review." If I were a sales manager again, I would define the strategy (albeit general) as follows:

Goal: Become the top expert in selling skills to drive my sales team's success.

Steps (no order possible):

- Take inventory and determine the top three for me and my sales team and focus on them by learning and training more
- Identify my own selling skills proficiency and knowledge for improvement
- Maintain my discipline to keep improving
- Participate in targeted courses, coaching, reading, learning, discussions, online sales, and management organizations
- Apply the necessary skills in implementing strategies through coaching, counseling, training, sales team development
- Review my performance and selling skill impact annually; make changes

In summary, your full-time selling days may be behind you, but being the master of selling skills for your sales team is essential. As a sales manager, trainer, and role model, they mirror your knowledge, skills, and performance to a great degree. Hopefully, many of your sales team members will exceed your selling know-how and performance. However, you need to plant the right seeds and set the sales skill standard for each salesperson's performance via hiring, coaching, counseling, training, joint sales calls, and role modeling—and do it every day. Continue to upgrade your own sales skills, introduce new, advanced skills you discover, and make sure you use your full menu to drive the success of your sales team.

7

Strategies to Align and Enhance Sales Motivation

THIS MAY SHOCK YOU, but you can't motivate your salespeople!

Contrary to the reputations of past "great motivators" Steve Jobs, Apple CEO, and Vince Lombardi, coach of the Green Bay Packers, you should recognize that no one motivates anyone else. Motivation is an internal drive, and everyone motivates themselves. Your salespeople are already motivated to sell, but some are also motivated to improve and master their selling skills, while others want to work independently, some want recognition, and many work hard for a potential "bonus." On the negative side, some salespeople are demotivated to prospect, manage their territories, be team players, or even to improve their selling with new skills. The good news is that the sales manager can help align desired sales performance with each salesperson's motivations, and even raise the level, or awaken a new motivation.

The motivation content that I will share in this chapter involves traditional motivational methods, and two researched strategies to surface/sustain individual motivations and help team members achieve their sales-related goals. Together, the strategies and techniques will help you improve overall performance and develop a more powerful sales team of achievers.

Capitalizing on motivation, and literally strategizing to help sales-people stay motivated at a high selling level, requires a broad, flexible playbook. First, you need to have a reasonable understanding of motivation in its deep, fast-paced, and invisible posture. Then you have to learn general tactics that you can use to encourage or enhance each person's desirable, sales-related motivations (hopefully, you can identify them). That's only part of the motivational game plan. Recent research has blessed us by pinpointing two of today's top drivers, and I will share how they can be applied to enhance motivation for salespeople. In addition, Porter Henry Co. has evolved applications to support these two "drivers," and I will provide tactics and tools as this chapter moves forward.

First, let's look at the big picture of motivation, and drill down to specific, general tactics to support each salesperson's personal motivations; later, I will share unique strategic applications that are focused on two of today's motivations, *Mastery* and *Autonomy*.

―――――

WHAT IS MOTIVATION?

Motivation, while powerful, is very challenging to fully understand and use to support your sales team's goals, ambitions, and direction. First, as you know, a person's motivation is extremely difficult to determine because it is dynamic, yet invisible, often totally hidden within a person's mind or subtle actions (he/she may not even recognize it). Second, motivation's level is difficult to pinpoint: How strong is it, how deep does it go, how long will it last? Third, a person can be motivated by a number of forces, and the motivation(s) can change quickly.

Yet, if you can understand motivation and the drive it can create, and do an effective job of individual salesperson research and observation, you can capitalize on it to improve performance without being a behavioral scientist. Practical and proven knowledge, in this chapter, will help provide every sales manager with a strategy and tools for supporting individual sales reps so they can capitalize on their existing motivations, and possibly awaken others. On the other side of the fence, when demotivation surfaces (failing to sell at a person's best), it becomes a huge obstacle that you can help overcome.

By definition, motivation is an intrinsic, intense desire that causes a person to act. People are motivated by different factors to take a variety of actions. As a sales manager, you can be comfortable knowing that all salespeople are motivated to sell, but what you don't always know is an individual's level and direction of motivation. Specifically, you want every salesperson to be motivated to sell at their best, get excited about winning business, be challenged by beating competition, and going the extra mile to achieve or to exceed expectations. You also want them to be motivated about their overall development and performance on an ongoing, career basis. As mentioned, the hard part is identifying what motivates each salesperson to perform better on the job.

First of all, everyone is different, and we often have different motivations. Secondly, those motivations can change very quickly, as can their intensity. A salesperson may feel charged up and ready to face any challenge the job offers after a bonus, winning a major account/project, or some form of positive recognition. That intense drive may not be there all the time, particularly when sales are off or the salesperson "misses her numbers."

Additionally, experts say that there are usually one (or two) dominant motivating factors that drive a salesperson at any given time. If you can key into the factors for each of your salespeople, you've got a foundation for creating a strategy to support his or her motivation(s). Motivation initiates from an internal source, but external behavior can often clue you in to motivating factors. To be a successful sales manager, you should be adept at identifying behaviors and try to learn more about each person's current motivations. With these concepts in mind, let's move on to traditional motivations.

TRADITIONAL MOTIVATIONS

Six common, traditional factors that motivate different salespeople at various times are:

Money
Opportunity
Teamwork
Independence
Visibility
Excellence

MOTIVE is Porter Henry's acronym for remembering the traditional sales motivators. There is no ranking for the six motivations, although money was, and still is, a popular driver with the incentive consultants. I'll cover them one at time in order.

Money

Money is the most obvious motivator. Money, or what money can buy, is important to many salespeople, but it isn't necessarily most important to everyone. Today, other motivators may be equally or more important. In fact, many sales and incentive experts have indicated that money per se has currently declined as a motivator.

Ways to impact and/or support money as a motivator include:

- Relate sales results to money (bonuses, raises, what money buys).
- Set up special incentives for superior performance.
- Discuss and reinforce personal and financial goals for the future.
- Help salesperson set financial targets.
- Reinforce financial aspects each time a sale is made.

I'm reminded of a "closing" sales call with Mary Jean, a young salesperson in her initial sales job with us. She was expecting her first big order and asked me to tag along. When the client handed me the order, he said: "I know what this does for Porter Henry Co., but what's in this for you MJ?" She instantly blurted out, "A new dining room set!" We all laughed, of course, but now, many years later in a successful consulting career, I trust money per se has been replaced for her as #1 by a variety of timely other motivations.

Opportunity

Many salespeople are driven by opportunity. What constitutes an opportunity varies from person to person. However, motivational opportunities usually fall into the categories of challenges, and the possibility of improving one's situation on the job or in life in general. When you've recognized this motivation in members of your sales team, you should try to create an environment or activity that offers opportunities.

Ways to create/foster opportunities include:

- Support and reinforce aspirations to be the best salesperson in territory/ district.
- Show how success leads to advancement.

- Provide for career-pathing where possible.
- Recognize and identify challenges in acquiring and penetrating difficult accounts.
- Delegate responsibilities that prepare the person for a future role in your organization.
- Set challenging goals, and explain why.

Teamwork

Some salespeople recognize and enjoy teamwork, and are perceived as hard-working go-getters who prefer to work and socialize with their peers. Coach Vince Lombardi claimed this was a huge motivation for his Super Bowl Green Bay Packers. Vince was quoted as saying his players were literally afraid to let their teammates down. The nature of a sales position attracts people who are independent and prefer working by themselves. However, there are many salespeople who do not fit neatly into that stereotypical image. They are motivated by the social aspects of being part of a team and contributing to the team's success, as well as the challenge of selling. These people may get satisfaction from team success, problem-solving, contributing to a team member's performance, being the number one district in the organization, or even playing a major role at a sales meeting.

If you identify this motivator as a factor, or foster sales team performance, you can generate higher team performance:

- Hold frequent sales meetings, phone conferences.
- Use sales competition with other teams to create your teamwork.
- Hold team social functions such as ballgames, cookouts, and so on.
- Get them involved in team projects.
- Suggest joint calls to allow them to learn from one another.
- Use "teamwork" and related ideas in your speech.
- Build in team incentives or challenges.
- Get experienced salespeople to work with inexperienced team members.

Independence

Contrary to team motivation, other salespeople prefer to be independent and are motivated when left to their own devices. This involves empowerment, independence, and freedom, enhancing feelings of power and control. This motivator should not be ignored or minimized because people belong to a team. Instead, use it to help independent salespeople be successful on their own. Later in this chapter, I'll cover a strategy on autonomy, which is, of course, related to independence.

You can:

- Delegate special projects or assignments (and then keep your hands off).
- Provide added responsibilities and authority (as it is earned).
- Have the salesperson conduct a segment of a sales meeting or lead the entire meeting.
- Encourage the salesperson to make her own account decisions.
- Trade off or publicize some reports of superior, independent performance.

Visibility

Recognition, approval, or a need to stand out from the crowd drives some salespeople. Whereas opportunity comes from internal recognition of achievements, visibility involves recognition from others.

- Give lots of approval for even small accomplishments.
- Provide frequent reinforcements.
- Applaud successes with a personal note and/or publicize to sales-force/upper management.
- Be sure salesperson knows accomplishments are recognized.
- Celebrate team and individual wins at every opportunity.

Excellence

Most people want to perform well, even if they aren't currently meeting expectations. The difference between the "excellence" and "opportunity" motivators is that the excellence-motivated person wants to excel at what he does and is not necessarily seeking higher and more challenging goals and opportunities. Excellence means the person takes great pride in achieving or surpassing personal and professional expectations, and in becoming a "master."

The key to sustaining and supporting this motive is contained in a behavioral theory called the Pygmalion effect, or self-fulfilling prophecy.

This theory states that your feelings about or confidence in a person's abilities will unconsciously be communicated to him or her via body language, actions, tone, and verbal interactions. If you are convinced that your salespeople are all capable of achieving their goals and you let them know it, this will reinforce their desires and motivation, and they will very likely achieve and perhaps surpass goals. Conversely, if you are doubtful that some people can't achieve their goals, that will come across and could lower a salesperson's confidence in himself. This lack of confidence may prevent individuals from performing well.

To move the self-fulfilling prophecy in a positive direction, you could:

- Establish personal and professional development goals and action plans together to enhance confidence that the salesperson will be able to fulfill them.
- Spend extra time with people who need help.
- Try to build on strengths.
- Ignore minor mistakes.
- Congratulate salespeople on their achievements and progress toward goals.
- Emphasize your commitment to his/her success.
- Convince yourself that he/she will achieve excellence and be positive in every contact.
- Establish expectations and communicate them frequently.
- Watch your body language—give positive signals to everybody.

TODAY'S TOP MOTIVATORS

Thanks to Daniel H. Pink, a best-selling author and researcher, today's dominant or top motivations have been researched and discovered, along with a plethora of ideas for supporting them. In his powerful book *DRiVE,* Pink identified and documented his interviews, research, and analysis with behavioral scientists and multiple successful business people, salespeople, and entrepreneurs.

As a result of his research, Pink identified what motivated many business people to succeed. Two of these drivers, which Pink named Autonomy and Mastery, with some selling-environment adjustments, are a solid fit with sales reps' motivation and ongoing development.

Autonomy, in this context, is working independently on a challenging task selected (desired) by the salesperson to solve a problem or discover a solution. Mastery is the motivation or desire to work hard and practice consistently, in spite of "pain," to achieve performance success. We'll further define and focus on these adapted motivation strategies later in this chapter.

Based on my understanding and analysis of his concepts, both of these motivators provide a great opportunity for sales managers to awaken desire within salespeople (if not active already) and to improve performance over time. These findings also resulted in the Porter Henry team developing tools for salespeople who are driven by either or both of these motivations. As a key part of each strategy, I'll cover how the sales manager can subtly launch these tools for the sales team so interested salespeople can utilize them to gain knowledge, skills, sustain motivation, and to improve performance. It's all about individual development and enabling performance growth.

For starters, Table 7.1 shows a comparison of traditional sales drivers and today's top motivators. They dovetail to some degree, but in terms of characteristics, Mastery and Autonomy are very specific, focused, and in-depth.

In Table 7.1, today's top motivators line up with appropriate traditional ones, although when defined, you will see they are specified, and defined beyond their traditional, general counterparts. Autonomy, for example, requires independence but gains its power by enabling the salesperson to find or select her own task or project to work on, one that she discovers and is challenged to find a solution for. And Mastery is not just wanting Excellence, but it requires the determination to

Table 7.1   Traditional and Today's Motivators

Porter Henry's **MOTIVE** (Traditional)	**Today's Top Motivators**
Money	
Opportunity	
Teamwork	
Independence	Autonomy
Visibility	
Excellence	Mastery

achieve success over time with intensive work, sacrifice, and constant practice, while overcoming setbacks and challenges. Pink defines the two motivations, identified critical characteristics, and validated each as a priority that individually has driven countless people to achieve success. Significantly, both of these top motivations line up with improving sales performance. Because selling is unique from other jobs, Porter Henry & Co. has made minor adjustments and focus to both motivators so salespeople can capitalize on them in the special sales environment.

The point is that the intrinsic values of MOTIVE, along with updated Autonomy and Mastery, are vital to many successful business executives and workers today, certainly including salespeople. You don't have to be a scientist or psychologist to manage your sales team, but it is important to recognize the drivers that underlie a person's performance. This knowledge will enhance the chances of success in implementing a strategy with individual salespeople that benefits each person, the sales team, and yourself, the sales manager. However, let's back up for a moment and look at the ongoing challenge of identifying each person's motivations before focusing on today's motivation strategies.

READING MOTIVATIONS

Reading someone's motivations and drives is like capturing a lightning bug in the summer at night—always challenging and sometimes impossible. In some instances, salespeople indicate motivations with transparent behavior or provide clues in conversation. With long-term relationships, patience, subtle persistence, and focused observation, you may get a picture of a salesperson's drives. This is where reinforcing the traditional motivations comes into play. You won't succeed with every salesperson, but over time, you will learn what drives many of your team members and hopefully you can enhance and support the motivation so it becomes stronger and keeps him on the right track to greater success.

Even if you can't identify the key motivations of a salesperson, you can still reinforce positive behaviors when they are demonstrated. If you fail in sighting the precise drive or drivers, in the process, you will still learn more about your team member, improve communications and relationships, and gain a better understanding of the person.

To illustrate the difficulty in reading and influencing/supporting motivation, here is a real-world example. Our company was doing sales training with a large, dynamic consumer products company, training their four different salesforce divisions. When we got to the National Account Division (mostly service, admin, some selling) of about 50 account managers, we were cautioned by management that most of the people in this division were transferred there over time because they had plateaued, had poor performance, were complacent, or near retirement, and basically lacked the drive to be effective. The business unit was known as a dead-end "graveyard" to finish careers.

As part of their training, we launched the same consultative selling program as other divisions, which measured product turnover, shelf placement, and out-of-stocks, all profit initiatives for both the grocery chain customers and our client. Not only did they absorb the training like other business units, but they took the consultative selling program to heart with exceptional success and significant results.

Equally important, I was pleased to learn that within a year or two, many of them (about a third) had moved up the ladder to new jobs and higher-level assignments. This was a perfect example of motivation enlightenment or renewal: a new program and challenge revived many of the account managers, activating many of the six MOTIVE motivations that we addressed earlier.

As indicated, there is no magic formula for reading a salesperson's intrinsic motivations. They're not easily or quickly identified, and this is impossible with some. However, there are methods for observing background, actions, and behavior as a basis for reading motives. They should all be used in concert to support and reinforce what you've discovered.

- *Search for the real salesperson:* Pay attention to the salesperson's behavior, personality, ambitions, lifestyle, finances, interests, hobbies, and family. The more you know about the person, the more you will know about what drives him or her.

- *Monitor behavior changes:* Any kind of change in observable behavior may indicate a change in dominant motive. A slacking-off in completing paperwork or making prospecting calls may indicate that there's a motivating force not being addressed. A salesperson who begins to develop outside interests or hobbies may be looking for new opportunities. Someone who joins a club or organization may be satisfying his teamwork motivation.

- *Ask the salesperson:* Discuss motivations individually with each of your salespeople and ask them to define the one or two motives or goals that are most important to them. Many occasions are available, including counseling, annual performance reviews, quota setting discussions, even over a drink after work. You may be surprised at the responses you get to this direct approach!

The bottom line for supporting and enabling the traditional drives is simply staying involved: (1) try to understand each team member's drives if possible, (2) frequently reinforce positive behavior to strengthen his skill and related motivation, and (3) quickly recognize a gap in performance and try to improve performance or behavior. Use coaching and counseling (the latter for serious shortfalls), particularly if you suspect motivation or lack of it is part of the cause.

In summary, these are motivation tactics that will help you manage better and with more confidence in the motivational impact. The strategies that follow, on the other hand, are ongoing for certain salespeople, who will readily accept them if motivated along similar tracks. It's the sales manager's job to educate the sales team and awaken salespeople to capitalize on the strategies and gain the success benefits.

THE SALES MOTIVATION STRATEGIES

The two motivation strategies, triggered by Dan Pink's significant research/analysis, will enable you to launch individual sales development plans that rightfully place the development success responsibility on each participating salesperson. Equally important, the choice to take part in either strategy is the salesperson's option, and that in itself will both enhance her motivation and chances for success. Development is personal, and individual, so the initiative belongs to the "owner."

Recognize that self-development is not normally a process or company policy. You provide coaching, supervision, and counseling along with other support activity, but the bottom line for self-improvement is how eagerly the person craves it and is motivated to pursue it relentlessly. Development is not a mandatory procedure but, like all "extracurricular" development actions, there are potential sales gains for those who take the right steps, along with other career benefits.

Having said that, I would like to reinforce the implementation and results to be gained from the two progressive, targeted strategies, mastery and autonomy. They are both beyond the traditional development offered by the sales manager or company. Development works best when it is self-improvement, ultimately applied on-the-job, and personal to a great degree.

To buttress this concept, and reinforce these priorities, *SellingPower* magazine's March 2019 issue features an article entitled "Salesperson Learning Performance," which highlights a study jointly done by the Sales Manager Association and Allegro. In brief, the study report indicates that most salespeople today want to learn and that 92% favored self-directed learning with priorities like shared best practices, peer learning (among themselves), and practice on their own time, preferably on the job.

This article reinforces mastery and autonomy as valuable learning applications. However, while both of these current discoveries add value to personal accomplishment and development, they lack "how-to" methods that fit salesperson implementation exactly. That's where a specific strategy, a concrete plan, featuring autonomy or mastery, comes into play with steps and rationale for launching them with your salesforce. As a result, you now have motivational strategies, with many benefits, that you can launch with your sales team or individuals.

The strategies also include some broad options, steps, and ideas for the sales manager to introduce self-development and possible ways to encourage or awaken interested salespeople. They offer broad, flexible routes for self-development, particularly for motivated, ambitious, or needy salespeople, to develop and sustain their skills and improve performance on a short-term or ongoing basis.

I'll begin by defining each of the two drives in-depth and how salespeople may use them if and when inclined. After the motivation strategies are covered, along with customized sales steps and tools, I will discuss the sales manager's role, primarily introducing and launching the concept to the sales team and letting the most ambitious reps run with a desired strategy. Certainly your coaching and development recommendations for improvement, reinforcement, empowering, or career pathing, will trigger the strategies and tactics that follow, and improve performance.

SALES MASTERY STRATEGY

Mastery is a desire for an individual to improve (master) performance to a high level, even though he may never achieve his ultimate goal. As indicated, mastery is certainly important to most salespeople today.

If used properly, it is a fabulous reinforcement and practice mechanism for applying the sales manager's coaching recommendations along with their own discoveries. Long-term, mastery will help sustain the right skills and enable the salesperson to be at her best when climbing the mountain.

Most salespeople want to improve, and mastery is a powerful, motivating solution. The challenge for many salespeople is that they don't know precisely *how* to improve, nor how to accelerate and maintain improvement on an ongoing basis. Consider the limited amount of coaching salespeople get, the resistance they face, the fact that a typical salesperson has to acquire about 50 selling skills (12 skills × 4 subskills), along with never-ending product/application knowledge. Wrapped together in a variety of different selling situations, this becomes a huge challenge. Further, each salesperson has to master the skills and employ them in a dynamic sales process. The skills and knowledge are challenged constantly and must be sustained in a myriad of sales situations, while avoiding bad habits that tend to replace or modify them.

Selling skills mastery is similar to breaking down the skills in a sport or profession like medicine or construction. You learn in a classroom, workshop, or study first, then get coaching and develop one step or tactic at a time, eventually putting them together in a coordinated activity, presentation, or work situation until they are synchronized and performed at top level. When you fail to continue the learning and practice, the skills vegetate quickly, are altered, and often disappear. If you think about a well-known athlete, musician, actor, or surgeon, you will quickly realize that their stardom and professional skills were developed by constant practice, focus, and improvement, in order to reach and maintain peak performance.

DRiVE identified a number of characteristics that successful people need to move toward mastery: deliberate, intensive practice for a long period of time; ability to overcome setbacks, frustration, and exhaustion; constant, critical feedback; repetition and reinforcement. These characteristics are also essential for salespeople who crave mastery. However, mastery-motivated salespeople, due to the challenging elements of the job and sales development needs, have to deviate somewhat with additional learning principles for their mastery success.

Identify Skill Strengths and Weaknesses

Few salespeople can "look at themselves in the mirror" and be objective. Coaching by the sales manager is very helpful and will enable them to identify one or more weak spots over time. Self-coaching after every call, using a Checklist for 10 Critical Selling Skills like the one offered earlier in Chapter 2, will be a great starting point. Repetitive challenges such as losing consistently to a competitor, or frequently hearing the same objection, should trigger learning needs that need to be mastered. Tracking data like prospecting, number of calls, and call frequency may point to a worthwhile improvement opportunity. The sales manager can help with coaching and counseling, but the in-depth improvement needs must be accepted by the motivated salesperson constantly seeking improvement.

Improve One Skill at a Time

If improvement is to be had, the weak or new potential skill must be given the spotlight until it reaches a satisfactory level. This requires intensive focus, and frequent use. For example, a golfer studies putting techniques and practices endlessly to improve; a tennis player gets coached on her backhand and works on it until she has the right motion, strength, and direction; a basketball player takes thousands of three-point shots until he achieves close to 50% success average.

Regardless of whether the salesperson is improving questioning, listening, handling price objections, closing, or a specific challenge like overcoming competitor X's new product, that needs to be the focus on every sales call where it surfaces. However, only one skill can be developed efficiently and effectively at a time, hence the disciplined focus. Verbal practice or role-play help along with ideas from others, but the targeted skill needs to be practiced and reinforced on the job frequently. Most experts endorse successful use of a skill at least six times before it becomes part of the salesperson's personal selling inventory.

Support with Extracurricular Learning

There is no limit on learning when seeking mastery of the job or skills. The most successful people are never satisfied and attend courses/ seminars; log into webinars or online learning; do role practice with peers; read sales books, industry magazines, and study; "ride" and talk with other salespeople; capitalize on sales manager coaching; and so on. The next productive idea or tip can surface from anywhere. Self-development and mastery should be implemented in many ways.

One of my very successful salespeople was almost a pest, frequently phoning in with questions or validating tactics that worked for her. My patience in her early sales days paid off. I soon realized that this was her way of learning, testing, and selling. And her intensity paid off, as she applied the ideas on the job, and eventually became a top-five national producer.

Mastery Practice Must Be Done on the Job

While it may seem obvious, "game time" provides the payoff for learning. Smart salespeople incorporate new ideas and improved skills into their sales call planning, and when finished, do self-coaching to assess how the improvement worked, then make adjustments if needed. Just as athletes measure performance with "batting averages" or "rebounds per game," it's easy for a salesperson to rank a skill's performance on a scale of 1–10 to track consistency in use and improvements. The salesperson can rank his focused-skill performance immediately after the call (while details are fresh) and document it to track improvements. Feedback and measurement are critical to improvements and long-term performance. Measurement and the success that follows are also great confidence builders.

Mastery, and its inherent desire and determination to reach a high level of performance, is a significant driver and motivator for many of today's salespeople, but they need to be awakened and provided with a path or structure. Wanting to improve is universal but following the mastery drive requires adoption of specific steps and frequency, along with a tool, such as a poster or flipchart, to act as a daily reminder, and to track and measure results. It is the sales manager's role to plant the motivation idea or awakening with salespeople who may adopt it, and support it with coaching, ideas, and reinforcement. Below is a mastery tool for enlightened salespeople who embark on a mastery campaign. The Toolbox (Chapter 10) includes the same tool along with instructions for use. Please note that the My Skill Mastery Tool includes the recommended steps for skill development, including focusing on one skill at a time, with a minimum of six sales calls, ranking skill performance, and tying in with feedback from coaching and other learning methods. It also mandates that the application series take place in one to two weeks so the "practice" calls are in a timely series to gain reinforcement.

My Skill Mastery Tool for Improved Performance

Describe targeted skill: _____

Select minimum six sales calls (within one to weeks); repeat cycle?	1–10 skill ranking for each skill performance	Notes on skill performance, improvements	Notes on sales call overall, account follow-up
1.			
2.			
3.			
4.			
5.			
6.			
7.			
8.			
9.			
10.			
11.			
12.			
Month's Analysis: # calls skill used: Improved? Not satisfied? Repeat cycle on same skill? Add new skill?	Average Score:	Summary Notes:	Next Mastery Steps:

Next Mastery Steps: Check via sales manager coaching, reinforce with role-play, outside courses, and learning; review skill when planning; move Mastery focus to a new target skill when you have mastered targeted skill.

SALES AUTONOMY STRATEGY

As mentioned earlier, Pink's research identified Autonomy as a top driver for many people in today's world. While different from Mastery, it is certainly related in terms of learning and improving performance (although less apparent), and offers other benefits. Autonomy is a desire, with freedom and total independence, to pursue certain projects, problems, and workplace assignments, with openness, to find a solution or create a desired project without interference.

As a dominant motivation in today's workplace, the autonomy drive has given birth to new companies, enabled businesses to generate new ideas and better processes, create solutions to problems, and gain greater efficiency. Equally important, it has enabled individuals to build their own skills and knowledge during the search for solutions. Entrepreneurs who are driven by the desire to build their own businesses and employees in many industries have temporarily gone off on company time to add improvements while developing their own skills and abilities. In other words, there is potential value for both the organization and the autonomy-driven person who often develops himself during the assignment.

On the surface, autonomy may not seem a productive opportunity for salespeople. However, with modifications and enhancements to the approach and steps, it offers significant benefits for the motivated salesperson, sales manager, and company.

It was determined that successful autonomy-driven workers or entrepreneurs need four essential drives or desires at their command. One was *Task*, the desire to discover a problem, need, or project to work on. Another was *Technique*, developing an approach, ability, or idea to finding a solution. *Time*, a third element, was often unlimited as far as working on the project. Selecting a *Team* to work with was also essential for success. It should be apparent to you that these uniform autonomy needs and drives, as defined, are not doable for the typical salesperson. As mentioned, the reinvented autonomy strategy for salespeople includes these four related drivers, modified to fit the typical sales boundaries.

The autonomy strategy recommended for salespeople has some changes to reflect the sales job requirements. Above all, it provides an individual project or challenge based on autonomy (with guidelines so he won't jeopardize his job), along with sharing parameters with the sales manager. The adjusted strategy still offers significant autonomy and independent freedom in terms of Task, Technique, Time, and Team. It provides potential rewards for the motivated salesperson, teammates, and the company.

Autonomy for salespeople may sound like a contradiction, since salespeople have more independence than most people in the workplace. Since an autonomy project often requires a deviation in time use or territory operation, it must be discussed, defined, and agreed-upon as a special project with the sales manager. Recognizing the need to define autonomy for salespeople, Porter Henry & Co. has adopted and enhanced some needs discovered in *DRiVE* using the appropriate name *START*. The acronym defines the parameter of an assignment that involves sales autonomy or freedom to pursue a project individually. The START criteria for the autonomy structure:

Situation—defines the project or task, conceived by salesperson (or jointly with manager)

Time—establishes a timeline for completion, time allocation

Action—determines how the project will be pursued

Result—what was learned, benefits gained

Team—feedback and how to share results so the sales team benefits

These steps are necessary to provide guidelines and to insure that the salesperson does not abandon his territory while pursuing a project. It also provides significant autonomy in planning with the sales manager and executing the strategy within the major guidelines.

Autonomy, as I have redefined it here, is definitely not for every salesperson. While many salespeople may be motivated to act on their own in challenging, desired assignments, some may not be motivated, or have the skills, to actively pursue a project as defined. Even the autonomy-motivated sales reps may not want to pursue this because (1) they want to focus on the territory 100%, or (2) they may lack the capability, creativity, or vision to engage in this kind of assignment. Consequently, autonomy as a driver should be defined and offered to individuals or the sales team as a development opportunity, but never mandated. In other words, the initiative for the specific task or project ideally should normally come from the salesperson and dovetail with his or her own development needs, interests, and motivation. A subtle, positive recommendation from the sales manager can also work. The true sales-autonomy project should not only be motivating for the "volunteer" but also have the potential to develop the individual's sales skills, knowledge, and experience and generate ideas for improvement of sales, skills, or related processes.

In implementing autonomy with your sales team, it is recommended that you present the concepts and tools to the team in a group or virtual sales meeting, discuss it further with enlightened individuals, and enable those that meet the START standards that follow to move ahead. I'll cover the launching of these concepts at the end of the chapter. Even the well-implemented autonomy project may not generate measurable or significant results, but in all cases, it will challenge the skills, knowledge, and experience, and support the salesperson's overall or specific motivation.

It is recommended that you launch only one autonomy task at a time within your sales team. Hopefully, success and recognition will motivate other sales reps to initiate a project of their own and perpetuate the process within the sales team.

Each of the five START implementation steps, a necessary structure designed by Porter Henry & Co., supported with a tool, follows in more detail.

Situation (START)

Once a salesperson has shown a desire to initiate an autonomy project, it needs to be crystallized to the extent that you can both agree on its worthiness. It may emanate from the salesperson or be recommended by the manager for skill or career development. The basic criteria for the situation itself are simple:

- It will benefit the salesperson (improve skills, knowledge, performance, and career development).
- It has the potential to benefit the sales team and company with new sales-related ideas, processes, data, and solutions.
- It can be configured to accommodate the other START benchmarks of Time required, Action(s) to be taken, Result (potential), and Team feedback.

Following are samples of possible autonomy situations or tasks for salespeople that may be generated by the salesperson, sales manager, or together as a team. Hopefully, the salesperson will come up with a need, or even modify sample tasks below:

- Spend a half-day per week with customer X learning their business so we can find new ways to provide benefits, applications, efficiency, and sales opportunities.

- Make X calls on accounts in _____ industry with the objective of finding opportunities/application for our products.
- Joint sell or coach (if qualified) with other sales rep(s) to improve selling skills and ideas.
- Perform value study with decision-makers on 20 sales calls to determine average savings per account.
- Screen new candidates for open territory during recruiting campaign.
- Plan and conduct a meeting (or phone conference) with sales team on how we can make forecasts more accurate and useful.
- Conduct onboarding training for new salesperson hires.
- Do marketing test for new product marketing.

Time (sTART)

It is important to determine how much work (territory time) will be needed to implement the situation or task. Obviously, you want to manage this carefully so the time allocated does not distract from sales production or territory maintenance. As a general guideline, I suggest that no more than 10% of the salesperson's on-the-job time be allocated to an autonomy project. Keep in mind that this timeline has many ramifications that need to be considered, along with related caveats:

- Assuming the maximum of 10% is a useful guideline, essentially this allocates to two days per month, for a limited period of time. The salesperson should recognize this and try to use her regular sales time (90%) more efficiently (and effectively) to compensate for the autonomy time allocation.
- The overall target for accomplishment should be limited, as well, and if a project is dragged out too long, it will certainly lose momentum and indicate, perhaps, that the salesperson is losing interest and may want to abort it.
- Most autonomy situations should be accomplished in the territory and may not take away time from the job. For example, working with a customer or series of customers to do research, or testing a better solution for an objection, will not diminish sales time to any degree.

- On the other hand, there are some situations that can be handled fully or partially on the salesperson's own time. Activities like planning, practice, or analyzing results can be accomplished in the evening or on weekends.

It's essential that you and the salesperson agree on the parameters so it doesn't impact on selling time, and ideally, can be done mostly on the job while selling.

Activity (stArt)

The Activity step is where the motivation and creativity take over so the sales manager should not influence this to any great degree. It should be reviewed with the salesperson, however, for these reasons:

- Make sure she has a plan for accomplishing the activity, rather than "shooting from the hip."
- Add any suggestions (if warranted), assuming that you do it subtly.
- Ensure that she stays within company limits.

Results (staRt)

You can't and should not try to predict results. It's important to have the salesperson share his vision for results, if available. Results are important, but they are not necessarily achieved in implementing every autonomy situation or task. Results can be achieved in many ways and the salesperson should be advised to track results in a variety of formats: data, experiential, third-party endorsements, and so on. It's important to recognize that results are of two kinds:

1. *Situation or task results*: Example—"Validated a prospecting method by using LinkedIn to qualify prospects"
2. *Personal development results*: Example—"Improved how to quantify and sell value to my customers"

What if the situation does not generate results, or if the salesperson aborts the project prematurely? While most situations will provide valuable experience, there is no guarantee that it will generate results of any kind. If minor results are generated from the experience or selling skills improved, then move forward to the next step.

If no results are incurred, or if the project is abandoned, then simply thank the salesperson for the effort, and encourage him to try again with another idea or autonomy challenge in the future.

Team (start**T**)

Team feedback is important since it is a means of sharing performance gains, building teamwork in general, providing recognition to the performing sale rep, enhancing, and adopting (hopefully) the new method or skill/knowledge enhancement. In addition to the project experience and recognition, it gives the salesperson an opportunity to present the findings to the team.

The key to team feedback is to encourage the salesperson to share any positive results; the sales manager makes this happen. There are many ways to communicate the results (with any documentation available) to help the sales team perform better. This support involves selecting the medium: telephone conference, brief PowerPoint summary, sales meeting, virtual Skype conference, or via email. The sales manager should facilitate this based on the salesperson's participation and provide a review or suggestions prior to the sales team communication. If the idea or improvement is substantial, it should be reinforced with a brief written recap.

The autonomy plan can be initiated by either the salesperson or the sales manager but must be approved by both. It will enable the salesperson to individually create or research new methods, ideas, techniques, and skills. In the process, the salesperson will develop his own abilities with the potential of finding improved or new methods for the company and the sales team. Regardless of success, this is a win-win for everyone involved, particularly the salesperson who will awaken and capitalize on motivation, fulfillment, and satisfaction to enhance her growth. It will build teamwork, as well.

Following is a tool (also in Chapter 10's Toolbox) to provide basic structure and to get a project started. If it sounds too directive to you or the salespeople, toss it, but maintain the START criteria. Remember, this is not a specific assignment, delegation, or straitjacket for executing it. The exercise is based on motivation to largely act alone and the only needed structure "to protect the innocent" are the five guidelines discussed. Use the Autonomy Challenge tool provided to jointly agree on the parameters.

My Autonomy Challenge Plan

Planning steps	Details on implementing the situation task
1. Situation (what type of improvement, solution, new ideas anticipated)	Task Objective:
2. Time (consider time on and off the job and ETC)	Expected Time for Completion (ETC): % of Sales Time Required:
3. Action (techniques or methods)	Description of How Accomplished:
4. Result (potential value of this effort)	Anticipated Accomplishment:
5. Team (possible benefits to teammates and how best to communicate)	Communicate Results to Sales Team: __Sales meeting __Telephone conference, Skype __Email feedback __Other:
Signed approval by both sales manager and salesperson:	Date:

Autonomy strategy will not be requested, adopted, or appear interesting to every salesperson on your team and it is certainly not an obligatory assignment. Indeed, some may recognize it as an opportunity and initiate a plan, only to drop it at some point. However, it has huge value for those who adopt it to improve and sustain performance, along with related accomplishments. Most important, the success of your sales team in using it will depend on (1) how you present the concept and format and (2) follow-up counseling and reinforcement that you provide.

AWAKEN THESE STRATEGIES FOR YOUR SALES TEAM

Launching, or awakening, these important self-development drivers with your sales team is the most critical step for ongoing implementation, sales team growth, and improved sales results. Simply "preaching to the choir" may get some activity adopted by one or two salespeople, probably top performers who need it the least. Similar to a "product launch," it requires planning, execution, and follow-up. To implement it successfully, follow these important planning and action guidelines.

Launching Mastery Strategy

Start with mastery strategy, since it is less complicated and will have a wider audience of potential adopters. Salespeople want to improve, but not all are motivated to work hard at it, and most don't know how to improve or have the practice discipline needed. You can launch mastery strategy initially in a sales meeting or phone conference by explaining the process and challenges, indicating the self-development value, explaining steps, providing a handout summary and copies of the tool, and answering questions. Don't forget to mention the "pain" of daily, long-term practice. Most important, get feedback from the sales team, including their ideas for implementation.

This open discussion will enable the team members to share their ideas more effectively on development, along with anticipated obstacles. Emphasize that the strategy aimed solely at self-development, and their decisions to apply the strategy, will often be optional and designed to improve performance but will not be mandatory or influence promotion, rewards, or recognition. The goal is to improve individual mastery and sales performance via proven steps and sales management support. You might emphasize that the steps are validated training concepts guaranteed to work but require continuity over time with deliberate practice to maximize results.

The salespeople who are driven to excel will surely adopt it. The mastery strategy is also a great follow-up tool after sales coaching. Remind salespeople with performance problems that they need to use the mastery tool to work on specific skill improvements. Be prepared to "demand" the strategy with the salespeople who badly need to improve, strongly recommending it as a solution for their development. You should also consult on mastery "deliberate" practice and monitor it using coaching to provide reinforcement. Periodically educate and follow up on the key concepts, use, and application. When engaged in coaching, counseling, reviewing performance, and sales meetings, use the terms and results in your conversations to maintain momentum.

Based on my experience in sales management and sales training, many of your salespeople will be motivated by mastery, but there is no guarantee that all will follow your lead and use the tool on an ongoing basis. The salespeople who use continuous, deliberate practice and follow guidelines to develop are destined to gain the most and are likely to become your future sales stars.

Launching Autonomy Strategy

I doubt if any sales manager will be able to pinpoint the ideal candidate for autonomy on his sales team: a salesperson who is highly motivated to work independently on her own project, has an idea to improve sales operations, and is requesting time and permission to find a solution. Not to worry. As mentioned, perfect candidates for autonomy strategy (redefined for salespeople) are rare. In real life, research defined the majority of autonomy-driven people as creative workers, executives who start and build a successful business, or others who come up with an idea, invention, or vision and gain freedom to work it into a successful process or solution. Obviously this definition leaves little room for salespeople to be motivated by the same opportunities. However, most autonomy-driven people are also motivated by challenge, recognition, excellence, opportunity, and so on, in conjunction with accomplishing the project on their own. This, to some degree, opens up the door for salespeople (and sales managers) to capitalize on autonomy. However, I suspect that you, the sales manager, will have to determine if you have salespeople with potential autonomy motivation in their blood. If so, there are many benefits for him, the sales team, you, and the company.

My recommendation, if you buy into the autonomy strategy, is to identify a salesperson who is performing at a good level (not necessarily your best producer), who seems motivated to accomplish more, likes challenge, and has a degree of independence, but is also ambitious for the recognition and may even desire future promotion or be a candidate already. Ideally, you have one or two salespeople who have these characteristics and appropriate motivation that can be awakened. When identified, they may be good candidates for autonomy.

There's some risk in offering this strategy to your team, since the wrong person (like a poor performer) may volunteer. Therefore, the best option is to assess your team and select a person(s) who reasonably fits the profile. Describe the opportunity (or need) with no other commitments than the motivational challenge and an opportunity to develop. Launching autonomy this way will surely help her to develop faster and capitalize on talent. After all, the autonomy candidate will grow in many ways depending on the goal: business acumen, marketing, efficiency, experience, management, and skills development.

You may recognize one of your salespeople, a person constantly coming up with new ideas or suggestions, even complaining about systems and process, who likes to be independent. If so, he or she may be a good candidate to challenge with this strategy. At some point, you may get salespeople who are motivated to reach out for potential solutions. It's very important to emphasize the benefits of autonomy for salespeople who are motivated to implement the strategy: enhanced learning and sales improvement, change of pace in the job, recognition, potential team or company benefits, and possibly management experience. There are also many benefits for you, the sales manager. The autonomy strategy can help you build your team, gain support to improve your reach with training and coaching, allow you to expand your team, and provide recognition for results and growth. And who knows what neat sales, management, or processes the salesperson may discover?

I unconsciously participated in a "pioneer" autonomy program as a rookie selling copiers. Rather than carry the 40 pound machine from door to door, giving demos, I multiplied prospecting by calling only with a business card and a quick pitch, returning at a later date for a qualified demo. When I became the top salesperson in the branch, my sales manager asked what I was doing differently. After he learned about my prospecting rationale, he asked me to conduct a branch sales meeting. Both actions enhanced my sales and leadership recognition, and I was soon promoted. In hindsight, this was autonomy in its earliest form.

In conclusion, motivation is a powerful force for successful salespeople, but a challenge to assess your sales team's individual motivations. Learning the traditional sales motivations, along with mastery and autonomy strategies, will bring you closer to each salesperson's desires and dreams, awaken others, and enable you to align and enhance them with improved sales performance. As a successful sales manager, you can confidently suggest opportunities to grow their skills, coach individual performance better, and provide invaluable support to keep your sales team highly motivated to achieve their goals.

8

The Strategy for Hiring
Future Sales Stars Strategy

LET'S FACE IT, HIRING new high-potential members for the sales team, often one of your timely priorities, really breaks down to two skills: (1) generating a large number of qualified candidates (recruiting) and (2) being able to accurately "read" a candidate's capability, goals, behavior, and past performance to predict success, and select him for your sales team. It sounds simple, but success is challenging according to retention data and the degree of success achieved by many of the sales team survivors. You should be shooting for the stars, and hopefully, you already are. This hiring strategy, if implemented fully, will minimize mistakes and enable you to select the best available people for your sales team.

In a perfect world, the sales manager has little turnover and successfully develops the salespeople that remain on board. Unfortunately, it rarely happens that way.

Sales turnover is a fact of business life, especially for salesforces where most salespeople lack proximity to the sales manager and daily supervision and are confronted with customer and quota pressures, long hours, and often travel feverishly. However, turnover is not necessarily bad, because termination of failed salespeople, if done early-on, has many benefits, both in terms of cost, time, and sales team morale. When it comes to salespeople who for any reason leave, we can assume they did not fit. Having said that, the successful sales manager must still minimize turnover and be prepared to replace departing sales reps along with high-potential new ones who are needed to support growth or expansion.

RECOGNIZE THE CHALLENGE

One of the most critical jobs for a sales manager is her ability to recruit and hire successful salespeople, or those with high potential. Hiring is the big problem, recruiting not so much. Selection is the major challenge and often the turnover culprit. In practice, the entire process is very difficult and time-consuming, validated by the high turnover in most salesforces. To underline the difficulty, the average salesforce has a turnover of 16% (CSO 2016 Sales Enablement Study); this means that some of the survey companies, based on averaging, probably hit high numbers like 25% or more! In all cases, it is testimony to the challenge of selling, as well. However, the blame for turnover is based on both hiring the right candidate, and then managing him or her. Most industry figures indicate that the average cost of replacement for one salesperson is about $250,000, including salary, training, lost business, and the sales manager's time. No sales manager can afford to make too many hiring mistakes!

There are varied reasons for making bad hiring decisions and some sales managers rarely emerge from these "rabbit holes":

- Pressure to fill a vacancy as soon as possible.
- Taking shortcuts in the hiring process.
- Inability to accurately "read" each applicant (when most are trying to present the good side only and obscure the faults).
- Not following a defined step-by-step strategy or procedure.
- Doing more "selling" than "asking,"
- Being influenced by a few visible qualities so that the "whole person" is never assessed.
- Hiring in the sales manager's mirror image: "He reminds me of myself 20 years ago"; "Alice's style is the same as mine"; "His aggressiveness and personality fit me perfectly."

The objective of this chapter is to provide a strategy with skills and tools that minimize and hopefully eliminate these potential problems; as a result, you will limit turnover while getting your share of the future "sales stars." Equally important, it will help you hire the most qualified people so that you can develop and manage them more easily, and of course, generate solid sales results. While training, managing, leading, motivation, and planning are all important skills, everything you do that contributes to sales team success starts with your hiring decision. If you hire right, development of a quality sales team is easier and certainly less dependent on your other management skills. Let's start with recruiting, the easy part, which basically requires commitment, discipline, and process. It's a numbers game, primarily.

RECRUITING

You can make the best selection only if you see the best available candidates—and only if you see enough of them. You should undertake a recruiting program that will produce large numbers of qualified candidates.

To protect yourself from having to choose from a limited selection, use multiple sources to provide a mix of reasonably qualified candidates. How much is enough? Interviewing six qualified people (selected from many more applicants/candidates) who meet the basic specifications should be considered the minimum number to ensure that you are indeed making a great *selection*. Even with six who qualify, your final decision after interviewing may be to start over and generate another group of qualified candidates.

Successful recruiters agree that the key to best selection is to recruit on a continuing basis. Recruit before the job opens up; always be on the lookout for a good candidate; and develop a file of good prospects. Then, when an opening develops, you have a starting point. You may even have the ideal person to fill the spot on your hit list.

Sources

In today's recruiting/hiring arena sources should not be a problem, but it's essential to broaden your mix in different areas. While you are probably being contacted furiously by online employment agencies, and websites like LinkedIn, don't stop there in broadening your recruiting efforts. There are many national online headhunters and newspaper advertising may reach a different audience. Also, don't overlook sources like community, state, military organizations and clubs like Jaycees, Kiwanis, and include college placement offices and job fairs. Friends and business associates can also provide good referrals. As the cliché goes: "the more the merrier."

In most cases, it's essential to talk directly with the person who will be sending applicants to you. Write out and discuss the candidate specs with sources so they don't waste your time with unqualified applicants. Also, set up a procedure for initial contact: get briefing by recruiter, provide resume, phone you for qualifying interview.

How to Qualify the Candidates

In a perfect world, you will get applications or résumés from perhaps 20 acceptable applicants. If you are fussy (admirable trait for hiring) or have challenging specifications for the job, many more candidates may be needed to fill your job. Therefore, it is essential to qualify the candidates either by reviewing their résumés or by speaking with them on the phone, or a combination of both.

Screening is an important step in the recruiting process designed to quickly exclude those candidates who are obviously unsuitable. At best, interviewing is time-consuming. Screening saves valuable time that can be better spent interviewing those candidates who have the essential characteristics to qualify for the position.

I said "obviously unsuitable" on purpose. Examples: an applicant has difficulty expressing himself/herself or one who does not have necessary experience. In other cases, the unsuitability may be less obvious and will depend on getting the right information as quickly as possible. Quickly weeding out unsuitable candidates will give you more time with the good ones, and will keep your application files from bulging with worthless data.

If you set up your recruiting so that candidates phone for appointments, or you call them after screening résumés, do some screening on the phone before making an appointment. A few key questions exclude those respondents who lack essential qualifications.

Ask questions bearing on education, job experience, valid driver's license, ability to travel, and so on, that are not apparent. Keep the questions and the answers very brief; then, if the applicant seems to meet basic requirements, make an appointment for an interview.

In the screening call, your purpose is to concentrate on the basic qualifications and, as quickly as possible, sort out the candidates you want to interview in depth from those you want to eliminate—*now*.

Use an applicant's résumé or application, if available, as a guide to asking questions about education and work history and red flags (omissions, high-risk qualifications). Caution: the screening call is not the time to sell the desirability of the job you're offering. There's no point in wasting your time.

The techniques of the screening interview are basically the same as those in the in-depth interview. The difference is in the depth of probing, types of questions, and the amount of time expended; for now, you're just trying to get enough information to make a preliminary decision.

Once a disqualifier crops up, don't prolong the interview. Ask another question to avoid coming to a sudden halt, then terminate the preliminary interview with a tactful send-off.

PLANNING TO INTERVIEW

If your company doesn't specify how many interviews should be given to each top candidate, take my advice and do as many as practical. At a minimum, this is two interviews for you, the sales manager, and one by a sales management or HR person with whom you can share critical results and responses.

Screening is a preliminary step to save time and eliminate the obviously unqualified sales applicants. Don't use this as a substitute for an in-depth interview. Be careful not to disqualify any potential salespeople on the basis of incomplete information or a premature decision. Prior to the first interview, make sure you do your homework analyzing the résumé or application submitted by each candidate. Don't overlook the basics.

Application/Résumé Appearance

An application that's "neat and pretty" doesn't tell us that the person is going to be a great sales rep. Nevertheless, some inferences can be drawn from the general appearance of the application, résumé, and cover letter, which may point to areas that should be explored in the interview. Here are some suggestions:

- *General messiness; failure to conform to spaces*
  - Poor planning abilities? Lack of thoroughness? Hard-to-control person? General sloppiness?
- *Illegibility*
  - Sales reports and forecasts might be hard to decipher?
- *Incomplete sections*
  - Applicant hiding something? Careless attitude?
- *Erasures and scratchovers*
  - Indecisiveness? Difficulty telling a straight story?
  - The entire application must be completed; attaching the résumé is not sufficient.

Education History

- *Longer-than-normal time to complete college*
  - Worked through college and highly motivated? *or* lack of application? slow learner?
- *People-oriented courses*
  - Courses in psychology, social sciences, English, speech, drama, and the like are more indicative of sales interest than, for example, physics or accounting.

Work History

How a person has worked in the past is the best indication of work expectations in the future. Some suggestions on judging an applicant's work history include:

- *Short-term employment dates*
  - Instability? Problems in interpersonal relations? Limited perseverance? Lack of ambition and career direction?
- *Long-term employment dates*
  - Eighteen months on a poor job might indicate conscientiousness. Five years on the same poor job perhaps signals complacency and lack of drive.

- Long tenure (with promotions and increased earnings) and/or success in a sales job are desirable traits.
- *Earnings*
  - Growth over time? Or little growth? Likely determines whether applicant was hard worker and well regarded, or demonstrated little ability, marginal work ethic, and lack of drive.
- *Reason for desiring change*
  - If some variation of the response "better opportunity" is used, check to see if the next job does indicate progress in responsibility, earnings, or both.

Red-Flag Areas

The recruiting and selecting process can never be reduced to mathematical formulas; there is always an element of risk. However, when certain factors are present in an applicant's background and work history, the risk is greater—often far greater—than average. These factors are called "red flags." Without indicating a need for automatic rejection, they do demand a strong need for in-depth probing during the interview. Here are some typical red flags that need to be probed or explored:

- Gaps in information
- Poor-quality résumés/applications
- Entrepreneur/family business
- Job hopping (i.e., four or more jobs in four years)
- Too long at same job (without any demonstrated growth)
- Earning need exceeds reality
- Number of changes in cities of residence
- Reluctance to provide information requested

Positive Indicators

- Referral from source you trust
- Lived in area for a minimum of two years
- Relevant sales experience/accomplishments
- Résumé suggests clear career directions and upward growth

What I have covered previously is pretty straightforward, and a great starting point if you have (1) followed the guidelines, avoiding shortcuts and (2) gathered a good size group of qualified people to interview. Now comes the challenge to your individual, personal analysis: reading between the lines, and data validation, ultimately making the best selection for your sales team. Let the real work begin with questioning skills that are essential for every successful sales manager.

The best salesperson I ever hired turned out to be my big mistake. When our Chicago rep retired with her first child, I interviewed a number of local candidates at O'Hare Airport. Mike was clearly the best candidate in every respect: bright, enthusiastic, charming, good sales experience, and so on. One red flag concerned me, however; he and his partner were closing down an unrelated, failed business after two years of struggle. It was a red flag I did pursue, but not in depth. Since we needed to fill the territory (after a few months vacancy), and compared to other candidates, Mike was a strong candidate, I hired him. He didn't disappoint us. He was a great addition and very popular with the sales team. More important, the first year he doubled the business in the territory, about $500,000; the next year he sold close to a million dollars! And then he abruptly resigned. Simply stated by Mike, he wanted to have his own local business so he could avoid the Midwest travel and spend more time with his family. I'm not sure if his family or owning a business was the key motivation, but he launched a small, local business and as they say, "lived happily ever after." In hindsight, my mistake at hiring him was not probing enough on his business failure, future plans, and even family particulars. Fortunately, my mistake was a trade-off for significant new business.

This mistake was breakeven since Mike was certainly profitable and built the territory, offsetting the cost of replacement. However, it underlined the red-flag concept, and convinced me, if there is one or more red flags, pursue them with in-depth questions and get completely satisfied with your research before putting out the welcome mat for the candidate.

Plan Your Questions

A recent conversation with Howard Robboy, president of Consumer Connection Inc., a successful national recruiting organization, reinforced the power of questions. I asked him what he believes are the keys to reading sales candidates, and he responded with some of the questions used to measure the "hidden" values, motivations, and shortfalls that we all have—the ones that are beyond traditional areas like prior jobs, education, skills, and so on. Here is his response:

> Ingredient number one—What are their long-term goals? How does that tie in to what they have done to this point? You have to start at the beginning. From where do they get their motivation? Is it their mother, their father, a grandparent? Did they work summer jobs? Did they pay for college? Did they lead on group projects? Did they lead through extracurricular activities? Did they start their own business in high school or college? Were they team captains in sport? How consistent is their drive and their passion throughout their career? Are they resourceful? Are they creative? Are they resilient? What is their energy level? Do they work out? Do they run marathons?

Howard then shared some of the critical, detail questions he and his team use to tie into the sales role and previous sales performance, which included samples like:

- "What level did you sell at?"
- "What were your year-to-year successes?"
- "How were you creative, thinking out of the box?"
- "What was your biggest sales challenge?"
- "What mistakes did you make and what did you learn?"

Questioning in-depth, with customized questions to fit your company sales job requirements is essential, and you can never ask enough questions of the qualified candidate. Behavioral questions and validating the responses are two big challenges. To help you, let's shift gears and add a proven process for interviewing and asking behavioral questions in series to generate in-depth responses.

Use STAR Questions to Assess Behaviors

If you haven't found out already, the toughest part of interviewing is validating the salesperson's past and future behavior, motivation, confidence, performance, competitiveness, integrity, and so on. Normal questions often fail to surface in-depth, truthful answers to these questions and that's where STAR questions come to the rescue when planning interviews. They will help you validate the personal qualities, behavior, and facts more accurately and supplement references, data, and hopefully, selling skills. You can also use them to test skills knowledge, although role practice, discussed later, is the best way to validate skill performance.

STAR is Porter Henry's acronym for a series of four questions that are asked in order (if all are needed) to dig in on specific behaviors or performance issues.

1. **S**ituation
2. **T**ask
3. **A**ction
4. **R**esult

STAR is a great tool for forcing a detailed response from the candidate, focusing on the four overlapping elements of a behavior or concern. As a result, you can zero in on sensitive behaviors or performance issues that are often "hidden" or altered by the job-hungry sales candidate. STAR methodology is not perfect in getting an honest response, but it is the closest thing to a lie-detector for determining the "real story," as in actual behaviors and thoughts, and thus predicting future action when the sales candidate might become part of your sales team.

Following are a few examples of the STAR questioning process used successfully by countless sales managers we have trained. These examples zero in on three of the essential behaviors for top salespeople that are often difficult to read during an interview: hard work, motivation level, and competitiveness. The same process can be used to determine or read other important behaviors for salespeople such as flexibility, pride, planning, integrity, and so on. When planning an interview, use your own words or our model ones. Here's how three of the STAR question series might look in planning an interview. The STAR Behavior Questioning Tool can be found in the Toolbox (Chapter 10) along with instructions for using it.

Star Behavior Questioning Tool

Candidate: Tony Thomas   **Date: 1/28/19**

Star questions	Candidate responses
BEHAVIOR: WORK ETHIC	
Situation: What personal, academic, or job situation paid off due to your hard work?	
Task: What were the specifics of the challenge or work and was it difficult?	
Action: Describe the extra work activity you took to handle the assignment? How long did it take?	
Result: What was the result of your efforts and how did you feel afterward?	
BEHAVIOR: MOTIVATION	
Situation: Can you describe a goal you set in business, education, or personal life?	
Task: Why was this goal important for you, what triggered it, and how did it surface?	
Action: How did you overcome any obstacles or challenges? What specific steps did you take?	
Result: What did you ultimately achieve and how satisfied were you with the result?	
BEHAVIOR: COMPETITIVENESS	
Situation: What's a competitive situation you have encountered in sports, or business?	
Task: Can you describe the situation and the competition, and what you competed for?	
Action: What actions did you take to compete? What worked and what didn't?	
Result: What was the result and were you satisfied?	

CONDUCTING THE IN-DEPTH INTERVIEW

A good interview starts with a good location. Select a location that offers privacy and freedom from interruption. This is most important. Remember, you're looking for spontaneous information of the kind an applicant would not plan on intentionally giving you. If during an interview, the applicant is about to reveal an important piece of information and is interrupted by a phone call, he or she may reflect on what was about to be discussed—and decide not to share it. So, whether you are interviewing in an office or in a hotel, be sure to arrange to have the phones cut off, and be sure people are instructed not to interrupt. Avoid restaurants and lounges so you don't have to compete with traffic and noise.

Check Your Interview Style

There is a range of interview styles, starting with an unstructured format, in which the applicant controls the subjects for discussion, going through intermediate styles, and ending with a highly structured style, in which the applicant is virtually interrogated.

The patterned interview, my recommended style, is characterized by:

- Planned, open-ended questions so that all important topics are covered and the applicant is encouraged to speak freely about relevant topics
- Preponderance of talking done by applicant
- Relaxed atmosphere

Set the Stage for the Ideal Interview

Setting a relaxed atmosphere is essential. It starts with your own attitude. Be warm, be friendly. Anticipate that most applicants will be tense and even apprehensive; but if the applicant is the kind of person you're looking for, you'll get a relaxed atmosphere if you lead the way. Start with a warm greeting; let your whole manner indicate that this may be the beginning of a long relationship—and it could be! Seat the applicant comfortably. You are the host and the applicant is your honored guest.

Show approval of the things the applicant says—if you can. If something is said that you can't approve of, don't let your disapproval show.

Handling this kind of interview is not difficult if you keep these tips in mind:

- Follow the plan that you've made for the interview.
- After asking broadly worded, open-ended questions, listen carefully to the answers.
- Emphasize questions that are based on *specific* past performance, tasks, experiences, and challenges, rather than general questions. For example, ask, "When was the last time you faced rejection from a customer? How did you handle it?" rather than, "How do you face rejection?" Use STAR questions to tactfully dig in!
- Follow up on any information given by the applicant that is vague, incomplete, negative, or unclear. Use questions such as, "In what way was it difficult?" or use a "reflection"-type question like "Difficult?" You must probe deeply and consistently to get a complete picture of the applicant.
- Maintain a receptive attitude throughout. Look interested, lean forward periodically, murmur agreement and understanding.
- Compliment the candidate on favorable data, and avoid any sign of disapproval toward unfavorable data.
- When taking notes, be brief and businesslike, not furtive. If you want to note an unfavorable item, wait until you are on to a new subject before writing.
- Bridge from one subject to another by commenting on the subject just covered and setting up the next. For example, "That must have been interesting going to the Region Championships. Tell me about your other activities."
- Don't ask leading questions. A leading question is one that "gives away" the answer. Example: "We need the kind of person who is a self-starter, who'll plug away all day, and not be afraid to make the extra sales or phone call at the end of the day. Are you that kind of person?"
- Speak naturally; although, if you're a fast talker, slow down the pace. The slower pace will contribute to the applicant's relaxation.
- Smile often, react warmly, be friendly.

Select the Best Candidate

As Yogi Berra was known to say, "It ain't over 'til it's over," and this applies to your final step in selection: comparing your top candidates and validating your best choice. The tool below will enable a simple comparison between finalists and move you closer to the ultimate decision, although there is a final step that follows; let's call it "validation."

Best Candidate Decision Matrix

Use this guide to compare candidates and make the best selection. Rate each candidate: 10 = highest; 5 = medium; 1 = lowest on a scale of 1–10.

Candidates comparison:	1.	2.	3.	4.
Factors:				
Education				
Work experience				
Performance				
Skills/knowledge				
Personal qualities, behavior				
How well each candidate will be able to:				
Deliver sales presentations.				
Build, sustain relationships.				
Meet or exceed goals/sales plan.				
Deal with customers.				
Plan territory coverage.				
Care for/use company materials/equipment.				
Develop knowledge and skills.				
Prospect for new business.				
Be flexible, accept coaching and change.				
Follow instructions.				
Get along with other reps in business unit.				
Be honest/systematic: expenses reports.				
Totals				

Validate Your Final Choice(s)

Final validation of your best candidate(s) is a must. Even if you have two "equal" choices after interviewing, validation, with reference and fact-checking, may tip the scales in favor of one. Be sure to check references, although this has become less safe due to HR departments protecting themselves against legal repercussions. We once hired a copier rep who seemed to have everything we required. His references from former employers checked out and were particularly reinforced with "glowing" letters from two past employers that he showed us. However, when his sales call activity and sales performance were consistently unacceptable, we challenged his work ethic and sales ability, leading eventually to termination. During his exit interview, he admitted that he had written the letters of recommendation himself on previous employer letterheads. Bottom line was that he was fired from both previous sales jobs for similar shortfalls that we discovered. HR had covered up the reason for his prior terminations. Checking references is important so do it diligently. Many firms today are afraid legally to disclose bad reasons for termination, and others will only validate employment dates. The best references are former bosses, not HR.

Selling skill validation can be achieved in other ways. One method to check selling skills is to set up a role-play in your office. You can have the candidate present her former product(s) while you act as a "buyer" in a typical sales situation complete with realistic objections. Another method is to establish a role-play situation in similar fashion by having the salesperson sell you a pen or other common generic product. If you utilize this method, allow little time for planning since you want to learn how well the sales candidate thinks on his feet and uses skills instinctively.

Finally, it's always a good idea to have the salesperson spend a day traveling with one of your senior salespeople under the rationale that he will be able to get a better idea of the job and challenges. It will also qualify his interest in accepting the job offer if made. However, brief your salesperson on questions that can be asked casually to validate information provided and to ask for feedback on questions, enthusiasm for the job, reactions, and so on. Validation doesn't take a lot of time or effort, but it can reinforce or even sink your decision, either of which is a cost-saving benefit.

Recruiting and selection is a very critical, risky, and expensive process for the sales manager so following a proven strategy is your best bet. A lost account, a blown decision, wasted coaching time, an unaccomplished priority, and delayed termination of a failed salesperson are certainly missteps in the life of the sales manager. However, hiring the wrong salesperson is the most costly mistake you can make, since it has many negative ramifications. On the other hand, recruiting and hiring a "lifetime" salesperson with star potential is a great challenge. Hiring success is a significant reward for the sales manager and a leap in faith for becoming a future sales leader. Regardless of whether you have high turnover or hire infrequently, when the hiring need surfaces, use these professional recruiting and selection strategic steps and tools to carefully make the right decision. It is the only way to create a powerful, successful sales team of which you can be proud.

The critical steps in short form:

1. Recruit heavily so you have a broad selection of prequalified candidates.
2. Plan every interview in depth, analyzing application and résumé to check on strengths and red flags and missing info; then develop target and STAR behavioral questions.
3. Conduct the interview in a broad, casual, friendly style until you have a complete picture and profile of the candidate. Have another manager conduct a similar interview so you can compare responses and opinions.
4. Compare best candidates using the Best Candidate Decision Matrix (Chapter 10's Toolbox), and make a preliminary decision.
5. Validate top candidate(s) qualifications by checking references in detail, assessing skills via role-play or field visit.
6. Make job offer and when accepted, after training, make sure to focus your coaching efforts on the new hire for three to six months.

9

Strategizing for the Ultimate Sales Leader

ARE YOU READY TO become a sales leader?

The good news: Once you have mastered the sales manager strategies covered in previous chapters, you will be closing in on the finish line of your ultimate sales leader marathon. The bad news is that reading this book alone is not going to make you a sales leader. Practice and application over time are the success factors. As you know, or should know, your personal development never ceases. This is particularly true for the sales leader because the sales teams, competition, and markets are always changing, along with new challenges. This, in turn, requires your sales manager and leader abilities to be constantly refined and developed: a true, never-ending marathon—achieving success with continuous improvement.

Before we move forward into appropriate strategies for the ultimate sales leader, let's compare, using Table 9.1, the two overlapping levels of sales management and sales leadership that I have hypothetically separated, primarily for learning/development purposes.

As indicated, there are significant differences between the sales manager and the sales leader roles as I define them, even though in real life, most sales managers perform all the overlapping skills and

Table 9.1 Sales Manager and Sales Leader Comparison

Key Elements of Job	Sales Manager	Sales Leader
Outlook	Short-term, day-to-day	Long-term, visionary
Style	Driving, selling, coaching, shooting from hip, reacting	Analyzing, thinking, planning, influencing
Priority	New business, managing team and sales activity, performance, results	Be role model, gain/build followers, achieve goals, drive sales team long term
Focus	Individual performance	Team performance
Major Compe-tencies	Need skills like coaching, counseling, selling, managing performance, recruiting/selection, achieving priorities, etc.	Thinking, analytical, planning abilities as fast-forward to the future, influencing the sales team, maintaining motivation
How Developed	Training, practice, experience, workshop learning, application, short-term development, ongoing practice	Training to establish foundation, continuous practice, experience, instinct, long-term development

strategies under one title or position. The bottom line is that to be effective in directing a sales team, regardless of title, you ultimately have to be accomplished in the overlapping roles since they are both vital for successful sales team performance. While I have defined the sales manager critical skills and abilities in previous chapters, this chapter will focus on three abilities and accompanying strategies that you need to master in order to be crowned as the ultimate sales leader.

The two sets of needs, while somewhat different, blend together in the real business environment. The sales manager is driven by actions and requires an inventory of skills to manage. On the other hand, sales leadership is generally focused more on abilities—long-range planning activities as opposed to day-to-day actions. Because of the challenges of daily supervision and failure of many sales managers to recognize the sales leader abilities, some sales managers are destined to stay in their comfortable jobs or function. Since most new managers are usually trained as sales managers per se with skills they can get their arms around quickly, they often build a career on that role. Consequently, many never become sales leaders unless they instinctively develop the abilities over time or get inspired by a proven sales leader, mentor, training, or hopefully, this book.

Sales leadership skills are less defined and often broader so I call them abilities, rather than skills. They often take longer to acquire. In brief, there are three critical abilities that the sales leader (manager) must acquire over time: *Sales Vision*, *Decision-Making*, and *Influence*. I'll cover these three vital abilities and strategies for each in this chapter. I trust you will recognize how they work together to provide sales leadership for the team. Let's start with Sales Vision.

SALES VISION

Business executives, employees, investors, and even consumers talk about the need for leaders, like the corporate CEO, to have vision, and to define and disperse a future picture of where the company is headed. The CEO's vision often includes a possible timeline, but little else. Most of us will have different opinions on the value of the CEO's vision: Does it work? How do you define it? Are employees following it? Do they understand it? Is anyone motivated by the vision itself? Does it enhance teamwork? Depending on many factors, the corporate vision can work to a degree or literally die on day one when communicated. Not so with the sales leader's vision—if implemented properly. Thoughtfully created and implemented the right way, it becomes a powerful strategy and driver for the sales team.

The sales vision for a sales manager, with direct salespeople reporting to him or her, is a great asset yet barely recognized in today's world as a defined strategy. We seldom hear about a frontline sales manager's "vision." And for that reason, the sales manager/leader's vision is relatively undefined and utilized differently. For clarification, check out two levels of corporate vision definitions, looking at the traditional CEO vision and my personal expectations for the ultimate sales leader.

The CEO's Vision

This is normally defined as the "place" where the company will be in the undetermined future, ostensibly being led there by the CEO. It's an opportunity for the CEO to put her stake in the ground and forecast based on a "vision" for the future. In rare situations, the CEO will add Goals, Missions, and a Strategic Plan for accomplishing the vision. In most cases, he will leave the details to others, which helps diffuse, distort, and ultimately bury the vision in history.

The Sales Leader's Vision

This vision is based on looking ahead to the future, analyzing and identifying marketing/sales opportunities that the sales team can pursue. It differs from the CEO's vision in a number of ways:

1. It's a realistic strategy, mission, or campaign, since the term is relatively short (often 6–12 months), ending when hopefully achieved.
2. The sales leader's vision is planned, focused, and measurable.
3. For execution to take place, it must be communicated and reinforced constantly.
4. It becomes a driving force—a goal—in the daily work lives of the sales team.
5. Strategic planning is required to make it work, along with implementation steps.
6. The sales leader's vision must be aligned with company vision and plans.

When effectively implemented by the sales team, the sales leader's vision (aka mission, or strategy) will accomplish the following benefits:

- Unite the sales team, build teamwork, determine a positive direction.
- Enhance motivation, extra effort, and focus from the sales team members.
- Challenge the sales team to excel and build excitement.
- Reinforce the sales manager's role as a sales leader.
- Combat typical obstacles such as competition and market or economy challenges.
- Become a strategy to create long-term sales success.

Following is a real example of a creative vision, implemented as a sales team strategy by its leader. As a result, the sales team enjoyed all of the aforementioned benefits and was instrumental in leading Porter Henry & Co. into strategic vision planning.

A Sales Leader's Vision and Successful Strategy

Larry Evans, a client sales manager, had an idea (vision) and developed a strategic plan to implement it with significant results. His company, a major producer of gelatin, had a narrow competitive market, largely pharmaceuticals, which used the commodity for manufacturing the exterior casing on capsules and pills. As a commodity, their gelatin was identical to industry competitors. All gelatin was purchased via an annual contract that was renegotiated each year, often on price. In an effort to differentiate themselves from competition, their marketing department created/identified over 50 value-added services (offered to clients without cost) to facilitate delivery and production for each account. The value-added services included items like parts replacement, just-in-time delivery, production machine repair, capsule design and logo creation for new products, special packaging, and so on. While these services were appreciated by most pharmaceuticals (great relationship-builders), they did nothing to alter pricing per se on annual contracts.

Larry's vision was to have his sales team quantify these value-added services, so it would give them a significant, concrete advantage for each account manager's annual negotiations. Obviously, they were not looking to use the values to trade versus pricing, but Larry recognized that if they could convert these intangible services into specific dollars, it would leave a strong, negotiable impression on the buyer's mind when trying to lower the value of their gelatin contract. He called the sales team together to get their ideas and buy-in. While some account managers were doubtful of it working, or even if it was realistic, others came up with ideas or questions. With help from marketing, Larry put together a method to quantify the benefits like downtime eliminated, cost savings, and so on.

Armed with a method to quantify savings, each salesperson tracked annual savings from just-in-time inventory, free service, and other cost-related savings for each account. Armed with this, he was able to rough out a six-month plan to identify savings that each account manager could use with their accounts (usually four to six) to track and quantify total annual savings. Larry drove his visionary strategic plan by constant coaching and communication follow-up to ensure 100% participation. Prior to the annual negotiations, the team met to compare quantified value-added services and to determine how they would introduce their worksheets at their annual negotiation.

The final results were significant. Larry's division was able to increase their prices 4% by capitalizing on the quantified value-added savings during the negotiation, and the following year, had a market-share increase of 9%. Larry and the team received recognition for their increases, and Larry briefed his two division counterparts on how to implement a similar strategic plan. Eventually, Larry became national sales manager. His vision paid off only because he and the team devised/implemented a team-driven strategic plan. In additional to the improved tangible results, the campaign focused the team in a challenging project, improved their individual performance and negotiating skills, and gave them company recognition.

Vision and Strategy, Essentials of Sales Leadership

Larry's strategic plan was creative and reasonably complicated. Strategic plans, driven by the sales manager can be launched at that level, or they can be very simple to be equally effective. Every sales manager has 20/20 vision, and it should be obvious that her sales vision must create and drive the mission with a doable goal. It doesn't happen magically, and takes time and thought and often analysis. Many sales managers get caught up in the day-to-day chaos of supervision, putting out fires, coaching, making sales calls, handling headquarters' demands, and so on. If you really want to become a sales leader, you must carve out time for planning—on the job or at night. Developing a vision takes opportunity analysis and planning without pressure from other sources. Fortunately, every sales manager/leader has the potential to capitalize on vision supported with strategic planning. Some achievable examples of vision for a typical sales manager/leader are demonstrated with goals like these:

- Achieve company product mix goals 50-25-25% for the fiscal year.
- Increase division market share 10% within 6 months.
- Acquire 10 new accounts, in $20K range, during Q1 and Q2.

- Contact all key accounts/prospects focusing on product X for a year, while Acme competitor is having mechanical problems, with goal of gaining 5 new accounts per sales team member.
- Achieve quota for branch by increasing prospecting level 12%.
- Capitalize on our new product line to achieve quota for the year by the end of October.

Strategic Steps to Follow

Fast-forwarding to the future, there are (1) unlimited opportunities you can surface, (2) goals and strategic plans to be created, and (3) missions and strategies to be launched and reinforced constantly. That's where the coaching and management of your sales team comes in. Let's look at the process and steps in detail for launching a vision and getting it implemented successfully.

Step 1: Create the Vision. Creating the vision is really about seizing (optimizing) opportunities. Opportunities are seldom obvious, so you have to make time for long-range thinking to find opportunities that are worth pursuing. It is easy to get trapped in day-to-day activities and problems, but *sales leaders make time for creative, wishful thinking and dreaming of what could be.* Visualizing the opportunity involves analyzing data, assessing your team capability and strength, searching for clues, brainstorming with your sales team, and conceptualizing. Much of it should be "feet on your desk" time to identify key opportunities and shape them into a strategy.

The following channels provide a framework for your visualizing. There may be other broad categories to stimulate your vision.

Where would you like your sales team to be regarding ...

- Sales standing/position within your organization?
  - Would you like to be #1 in your region?
  - Or perhaps in the top 10 in the organization?
  - #1 in new product sales?
  - Is your team ready to be challenged and grow?
- Your competition in your marketplace?
  - Do you see your team as being #1 versus competition in your marketplace?

- Do you see your team building market share?
- What are competitive strengths and weaknesses?
- Profitability?
  - Would you like to be the most profitable district in the region?
  - Do you see yourself as improving your profitability picture substantially in some way?
- Rewards/recognition?
  - Do you see your team gaining recognition? Perhaps through awards, incentives, or bonus for sales growth or other performance?
  - Overall, what drives your team, and how can you capitalize on it?

> Constantly ask yourself: Where do you want your sales team to be?

Step 2: Convert Sales Vision into Goals. The next step in developing a sales vision is to focus the broad vision you have identified by converting it to one or more goals. The more specific your goal, the easier it will be to communicate it to the team and the easier it will be for the team to understand it, commit to it, and work toward it. *Think of the goal as your objective, or your destination. You can't develop a strategy without it.*

You are surely familiar with SMART goals, but in any case, take a minute or two to review the five standards of the SMART acronym:

1. *Specific:* Specify precisely what you want to accomplish within the given time frame. Provide enough detail so no one will lack understanding of the big picture.
2. *Measurable:* Will you be able to tell when you've achieved it, or have made progress toward the goal? Use numbers like dollars, percentages, units, quotas, and the completion dates to make your goal measurable. This will help you track progress and identify problems as you proceed.
3. *Aligned:* Each goal should be aligned with, or, at minimum, not conflict with your organization's goals and values, and corporate vision.

4. *Realistic:* Build stretch into the goals you set for the sales team, but be sure they're doable. Given present and predictable future circumstances, try to make certain the goal is attainable, considering available resources such as time, information, budget, people, and so on. If the goal is beyond the ability of the team, the team will become frustrated instead of challenged.

5. *Time-bound:* Specify a target date for accomplishment of each goal.

Step 3: Develop Strategies. Strategies describe how you will achieve the goals. They describe the overall game plan or approach to achieve the goals.

For instance, in pursuit of your goals, perhaps your strategies will call for your team to:

- Find new product applications with accounts and prospects.
- Increase your account base or build sales X%.
- Manage and grow relationships within existing accounts.
- Create urgent needs to sell/launch a new product.
- Upgrade and enhance motivation and training of the sales team regarding an old product.

Step 4: Identify Tactics. The fourth step in developing your sales vision is to identify tactics. Now that you know where you want to go, what you need to achieve, and how you are going to get there, you need to identify specific action steps that will propel the team. You can consider your sales vision goal the destination and the tactics your road map.

In determining your tactics keep these ideas in mind:

- *Identify major activities or benchmarks.* Just as you would note landmarks on a road map, you should identify key points and activities in your action plan to be sure you're on the right track and are headed toward your destination.
- *Define responsibilities and other resources needed.* Each team member should play a defined role in carrying out tactics and helping to achieve the sales vision goals. To ensure successful completion of individual tactics, be clear and specific in defining responsibilities and how they will be carried out. Identify necessary resources and include them in the action plan.

- *Specify target dates for completion.* In order to move closer to your goal and reach it within the designated time frame, set target dates for each action step. Target dates also create a sense of urgency and motivate the team to move ahead together.
- *Sequence the tactics chronologically from launch to completion.* Tactics should be listed in the order in which they are to be completed and should indicate any relationships between steps.
- *Construct a tactical action plan for each strategy you develop.* This will clarify for you and everyone else just what is required to implement each strategy successfully.

Following is a strategic planning format for developing a vision into a workable plan, with vision, goal, actionable tactics, timetable, and more. I call it a VisiPlan for obvious reasons.

Visiplan

Date: 1/10

Vision

Where do you want to be?
To be the #1 sales district in the region by end of year, exceeding sales quota, achieving product mix, capitalizing on good economy, and hiring experienced sales team

Goals

What will you need to achieve to get there? Make the goals SMART: specific, measurable, aligned, realistic, time-bound
- Increase sales volume 20% by June 30.
- Achieve Company product mix goals (Product A 40%, Product B 30%, Product C 30% by June 30).
- Increase our market share (versus competition) by 5% by June 30.
- Hire experienced salesperson for new territory during Q1 if possible.

Strategies

How will you achieve your goals? What is your overall approach?
- Increase sales coverage.
- Run volume and product mix special incentive programs for sales team.
- Demonstrate competitive advantage to customer base, especially Product C where competition is most vulnerable.

- Open a minimum of 10 new accounts each quarter.
- Allocate the quarterly new account expectations based on each rep's past performance and territory potential.

Action plan	Responsibility	Target date
1. Work with marketing dept. to identify competitive advantages in written report.	Me, Jane P. (mktg. VP), Marco (product C mgr.)	January 1
2. Devise special sales literature for Product C.	Me, marketing (Marco), Janet (art dept.)	January 31
3. Develop local list of customer references.	Sam, entire sales team	January 31
4. For Product C, set conversion goals with sales team.	Sales team	January 14
5. Train sales team in selling against competition via questioning, handling resistance, and using sales literature.	Sue, training dept., Me, Kim, #1 sales rep, set up phone conferences as needed	February 30
6. Follow up/coach each salesperson on minimum of two coaching visits per sales quarter.	Me	February 1 – ongoing
7. Review progress/obstacles at weekly phone conference and monthly sales meeting.	Me, sales team	Ongoing
8. Start recruiting and interviewing experienced account manager for open territory.	Me with support from HR and boss	January 15, complete hiring and onboard by March 31

If creating a sales vision for the team, doing the analysis and building a strategic plan sounds like a lot of work to you, you are right. But that's one of the main hurdles that distinguishes a sales leader from a sales manager. However, the job continues to be tough in communicating the plan and getting it implemented. Now for step 5.

Step 5: Communicate, Communicate, Communicate. Now that you've spent weeks or months designing a plan to implement your vision, send it to your salespeople. Wrong! Actually they should be involved in the design and development of the plan all along—give them a piece of the ownership and gather better ideas than your own single viewpoint. After all, the sales team is on the frontline battling competition and obstacles every day and the sales reps may know where the opportunities are or provide clues.

Getting the sales team (and others, including management) involved is just the beginning and now you have to make it happen—implementation, that is. You know how to communicate, so I won't add a lot of "how to" verbiage. However, following are a few suggestions to mobilize your team and get them to collaborate 100% (or more):

- Launch it at a sales meeting or phone conference with a big bang. Give credit to the team for contributions and ask for added ideas, since this is an ongoing, growing plan; discuss some of the challenging strategies and tactics; answer questions and concerns. Above all, stress teamwork and the ultimate rewards for success.

- Frequently reinforce the plan or elements of it. Follow each salesperson's schedule, timetable, and performance to make sure they value the plan and are fully contributing. Listen to suggestions and make changes if needed. Make sure everyone stays on target.

- Communicate results to motivate the team. Be prepared to celebrate and capitalize on every significant success. Use email, phone, coaching visits, and conferences to frequently communicate and always buttress the plan itself.

The right vision and plan communicated consistently will motivate the team with a common target and path to get there. It's all about success, and if done smartly and carefully, your vision will improve performance and sales results, often dramatically. Your vision is one key to sales leadership, but communication alone will not get the vision successfully implemented. The segment on *Influence,* later in this chapter, will reinforce and add other methods for positive communication and follow-up, and so will the next segment on a decision-making strategy. A blank copy of the VisiPlan, along with supporting instructions, can be found in the Toolbox (Chapter 10). Use it as a model for your vision.

Is Your Vision 20/20?

Let's back up for a few minutes and do a reality check on your vision and your tendency to take action on strategic or other opportunities. Following is a validated assessment that will provide feedback on your ability to create a vision, and equally important, your motivation/instinct to take action and capitalize on the potential opportunity. The assessment will also measure your risk-taking tendencies. After you complete the assessment, take a few minutes to review your results with the scoring instructions that follow.

Vision/Risk Leadership Indicator

INSTRUCTIONS: The following exercise, consisting of 40 questions and situational decisions, is designed to identify and profile your vision and risk abilities. It is not a personality test, and there are no "right" or "wrong" answers. If you respond to the questions/situations objectively, you will receive accurate feedback on some of your leadership strengths and abilities.

To complete the exercise, simply circle "A" or "B" for each of the 40 questions/ situations based on which choice is closest to your actual preference, or which indicates most accurately how you would react in a real-life situation. As a scoring alternative, number a blank piece of paper 1–40 to track your responses. Complete all 40 questions/situations as quickly as possible and do not omit any; don't overanalyze the choices. When you have finished the exercise, complete the chart that follows to gain an explanation of what it means and how this profile can help you develop your leadership abilities.

You are now ready to begin. Please respond to every question or situation frankly. Don't waste time looking for hidden meanings.

1. In your present job, which would you prefer?
   A. More time to get the immediate high-priority tasks accomplished.
   B. More time to step back and see where you and your staff are heading and do some long-range thinking.

2. You are driving a car approaching an intersection with a green light. When you are 25 feet away, the light turns yellow. Would you normally:

   A. Stop?

   B. Try to "beat" the light before it changes to red?

3. You've just been confronted with a tough business problem and have evaluated all the options but can find no "ideal" solution. What would you do?

   A. Select the best option and go with it.

   B. Stick with the problem and search extensively for the right answer.

4. You are at the racetrack waiting for the last horse race to begin. You are ahead for the day by $500 and plan to bet it all on the last race. Would you bet on:

   A. The favorite with even odds?

   B. An underdog at 10–1 odds?

5. Given the choice of another career, which would you choose to be?

   A. A scientist, physician, or technologist

   B. An actor, artist, or musician

6. You have just completed interviews with two finalists for a key position on your staff. What is your decision?

   A. Hire staffer "X," who has proven credentials and experience, but whom you feel may be limited in potential.

   B. Hire candidate "Y," who has unproven credentials, yet shows plenty of potential.

7. Which type of work do you prefer?

   A. Dealing with straightforward problems where there are specific answers and measurable results.

   B. Working on complex issues, often conceptual in nature.

8. You're making some last-minute changes on an important project. You also have other priorities to attend to. Would you normally:

   A. Work overtime and do both tasks yourself?

   B. Delegate the other priorities to a staffer?

9. You are about to receive a major promotion. Your boss has provided you with a choice of two jobs, each offering equal pay and opportunity but affording different challenges. Which would you accept?

   A. The production department where your performance would be measured in terms of units produced, efficiency, cost control, and so on.

B. The advertising department, where your performance would be measured on the basis of creativity, ideas, and your ability to understand concepts and create an image that meets intangible and subjective standards.

10. You are purchasing a house. Assuming that values and costs are equal, and that time is not a factor, which would you choose?

    A. A resale house you can see and tour, which will require some repairs, painting, and refurbishing.

    B. A house in the blueprint stages that will force you to rely on the builder's reputation.

11. How would you describe yourself?

    A. I behave according to accepted codes of conduct and values.

    B. I like being recognized for my individuality and uniqueness, even if it means being conspicuous at times in terms of dress and behavior.

12. One of your better-performing subordinates is, according to a confidante, looking for another job. Your best approach in this instance would be to:

    A. Do nothing. If she's unhappy, there's little you can do.

    B. Counsel him to find out what the problem is, even if this may have a negative effect on the outcome.

13. Would you prefer your business associates and friends to think of you as:

    A. Someone who relies on proven practices in order to solve problems?

    B. A person who takes an unorthodox approach to problem-solving?

14. You've recently generated a great idea to save your company a significant amount of money and most people you've shared it with agree. However, your boss thought that the idea was impractical. Your move in this situation should be:

    A. Discard or change the idea.

    B. Go over your boss's head, even if he/she gets annoyed.

15. Which of these describes your habits?

    A. Keeping a consistent, steady pace.

    B. Working in short bursts of energy and enthusiasm.

16. Do you prefer:

    A. Working with people who are orderly, disciplined, and thoroughly reliable?

    B. Working with people who are creative, spontaneous, and challenging, but who may be difficult to manage?

17. Which of the following characteristics most accurately describes your managerial style?

    A. Detail-oriented.

    B. Overwhelmed by too much detail.

18. Which saying best suits a competitive business situation?

    A. "Look before you leap."

    B. "He who hesitates is lost."

19. You have analyzed two business opportunities for your company, which appear to be equal in terms of cost and potential. Opportunity "A" is logical and practical, but your "sixth sense" tells you that "B" is the way to go. What would be your choice?

    A. Opportunity "A," where your existing skills and knowledge can produce solid results.

    B. Opportunity "B," which provides change, challenge, innovation, and the opportunity to explore new and unknown opportunities.

20. You are pressured to make a major decision. You have analyzed the options but have reached an impasse. In this situation, your best bet is to:

    A. Go to your boss, present him or her with the final options, and let him or her make the decision.

    B. Pick the one that you feel will work.

21. How would you describe the goals you normally set for yourself and others?

    A. Realistic, practical, and achievable.

    B. Very ambitious.

22. You are coaching a college football team competing for the national championship. Your team has just scored its only touchdown, making the score 7-6 in favor of your opponent. There's time for one more play. Which strategy would you implement?

    A. Kick for the extra point and a tie. Your kicker has not missed a single extra point all season and it's a sure thing.

    B. Go for the two-point conversion since your team has made 50% of its two-point conversions all season.

23. How do you like people to think of you?

    A. As someone who get his/her facts straight.

    B. As an "idea" person.

24. Which situation would make you happiest?

    A. You inherit $100,000 from a rich uncle.

    B. You earn $100,000 in the stock market by investing $10,000 in a company that takes off.

25. Have you ever accomplished anything (in business or your personal life) that other people thought was not possible?

    A. No.

    B. Yes.

26. You learned that several commercial building developers are seriously looking at undeveloped land in a certain location. You are offered an option to buy a choice parcel of land. The cost is about two months' salary, and you calculate the potential gain to be 10 months' salary. Would you:

    A. Let it slide—it's not for you?

    B. Purchase the land?

27. How would you describe yourself?

    A. A person with both feet on the ground.

    B. Someone who is frequently dissatisfied and looks for new ways to do things.

28. You are competing with two people on a game show and can choose one of the following. Which would you choose?

    A. $1,000 in cash.

    B. A one-out-of-three chance of winning $15,000.

29. You've developed what you think is a very exciting and effective opportunity for your company that you'd like to implement with your own staff. Your boss is "lukewarm" to the concept, and some of your staffers don't seem to understand the value of your proposal. Would you:

    A. Abort the project because you have no support?

    B. Use influence to get your boss and staff more excited about the possibilities?

30. The apartment building where you live is being converted to condominiums. You can either buy your unit for $80,000 or sell the option for $20,000. The market value of the condo is $120,000. You know that if you buy the condo, it might take six months to sell. The monthly carrying cost is $1,200, and you'd have to borrow the down payment for a mortgage. You don't want to live in the building. What do you do?

    A. Take the $20,000.

    B. Buy the unit and then sell it on the open market.

31. Have you ever had an idea that you never fully pursued that turned out to be a "winner" for someone else?

    A. No.

    B. Yes.

32. You've come up with a great idea for a new product, which can be protected by copyright. All of your friends think it's terrific and something that can't miss. What would you do?

    A. Accept an offer of $100,000 from a company that's very interested in producing and marketing your product and wants to purchase the rights to it.

    B. Start your own company (assuming you can raise sufficient capital from friends and backers).

33. Which of the following statements do you feel is more accurate?

    A. Common sense is more important in management than vision.

    B. Vision is more important in management than common sense.

34. You've lost $500 at a blackjack casino. How much are you prepared to gamble in order to win the $500 back?

    A. Nothing.

    B. $250.

35. Which of these statements describes you best?

    A. I am most comfortable when I think and act in practical, specific ways—where there are tangible outcomes.

    B. I am a conceptual thinker who enjoys theories and abstract ideas.

36. You work for a small, yet thriving, privately held electronics company. The company is raising money by selling stock to its employees. Management plans to take the company public, but not for four more years. If you buy stock, you will not be allowed to sell until shares are traded publicly. In the meantime, the stock will pay no dividends. But when the company goes public, the shares could trade for 10–20 times what you paid for them. How much of an investment would you make?

    A. None at all.

    B. One month's salary.

37. Select the answer that most accurately describes you and your work:

    A. During the last year, I've initiated less than four major changes (procedures, plans, and projects) in my job.

    B. During the last year, I've initiated more than four major changes (procedures, plans, projects) in my job.

38. A month after you purchased it, the value of your investment suddenly skyrockets by 40%. Assuming you can't find any further information, what do you do?

    A. Sell it.

    B. Hold it on the expectation of further gain.

39. You could best be described as:

    A. A "Renaissance" person—one with a wide breadth of interests, who likes to get involved in many things and a variety of projects.

    B. An obsessive, single-minded, and focused person who likes to get involved with one mission or task at a time in order to get it accomplished right.

40. Your mutual boss, who is unaware of a severe personal problem that has had a negative impact on your friend's performance, has given this friend a bad performance review. You should:

    A. Mind your own business and not get involved.

    B. Tell your boss the facts even though it might hurt your relationship with either of the two.

Now, score your effort.

Sales Management Success: Optimizing Performance to Build a Powerful Sales Team.
Copyright © 2019 by Warren Kurzrock. All rights reserved.

Scoring

The scoring mechanism for the Vision/Risk Leadership Indicator has been designed so that you can interpret it easily and quickly. In brief, the following is your guideline to scoring:

- The 20 *odd* questions and situations (1, 3, 5, 7, etc.) are indicators of *vision*.

- The 20 *even* questions and situations (2, 4, 6, 8, etc.) are indicators of *risk-taking*.

- The "B" choices *only* count as score indicators for each question/situation.

To determine your score, add all the odd "B" choices and even "B" choices. For example, you may have selected "B" for 9 odd-number questions and 12 even-number questions.

I selected "B" for _____ odd-numbers questions. (This number indicates your Vision Profile.)

I selected "B" for _____ even-number questions. (This number indicates your Risk Profile.)

Interpretation of Your Score

The Vision/Risk Leadership Indicator measures two important and interacting leadership abilities. A true sales leader must have vision and be capable of taking calculated risks.

The easiest way to illustrate the concept and position scores is to use the grid that we have provided below. The scores are plotted along each axis, which contains a range of 20 points. It should be apparent that the midway point is 10, and a "perfect" score is 20. However, it should be noted that someone who indicates a 20 in both Vision and Risk might not be the "perfect" leader. While "20/20" vision is ideal (few people have it), a 20 on risk-taking is dangerous. That's why there's a "danger zone" in the grid—to emphasize the fact that anyone who falls in this zone, or very close to it, should be aware that he or she is probably a heavy risk-taker.

To determine your Vision/Risk Profile, plot your combined scores on the grid in Figure 9.1. For Vision (odd questions), go up the vertical axis; for Risk (even questions), go along the horizontal axis (bottom).

High Vision/Calculated Risk is the ideal quadrant for the sales leader's score. *Low Vision/Low Risk,* on the other hand, is a poor place to be because it indicates a comfort level, or complacency, and little

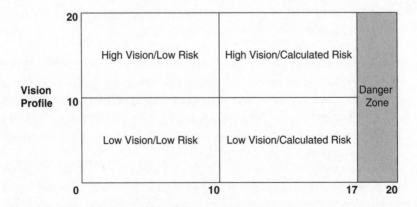

Figure 9.1   Vision/Risk Grid

concern about looking forward and taking appropriate actions. If you scored in either of the other adjacent quadrants to *High Vision/ Calculated Risk,* it indicates you need to work on the appropriate skill, improving vision or being more active to capitalize on vision opportunities. Most important, if you wound up in the gray *Danger Zone,* the message is that you have a tendency for risk-taking and need to be more cautious. The bottom line for this exercise is to look for opportunities (vision), analyze them, and act on those that are doable and minimize risk. Taking actions with the best opportunity and calculated risk is the ideal way to achieve success.

Hopefully, you are positive about your sales leadership feedback. Even if you were unhappy, the tool indicates where you need to be to become an accomplished sales leader. So, go for it! Let's move on to another essential strategy, decision-making, often related to sales leadership ability,

---

DECISION-MAKING

As a sales manager, you have already experienced the importance of making decisions. And you probably have made some good decisions along with some bad ones. Moving to sales leader status, you need to have a good batting average for making the "right" decisions at the right time and often dealing with more serious, complicated ones. Poor decisions or delayed ones subtly endanger your leadership credentials. In contrast, good, timely decisions encourage your sales team to follow your direction, to stretch their performance, to take pride in the team efforts, and simultaneously enhance respect for you. Good decision-making is critical for any sales manager, but it is essential for every sales leader's success.

As a sales manager or sales leader, you will never make powerful decisions like President John Kennedy's outstanding decision to put a man on the moon; in contrast, his equally memorable failed decision was the "Bay of Pigs" disaster. Similarly, consider Hillary Clinton's career of making many good decisions only to let some poor decisions (failing to focus on "jobs" in a few "needy" states and employing a private email system) hurt her presidential campaign. Sales managers/ leaders like us are not at that level, of course, but decision-making is just as important for our success. The point here is that decision-making, at any level, both good and bad, has significant impact on leadership, respect, influence, and success. For the sales leader, good decisions are important in moving forward, and bad decisions deter progress. Equally important, both are visible to the sales team and will impact your ongoing sales leadership.

While most sales leaders have a direct authority over the sales team, with both serious and less important decisions, decision-making can motivate or demotivate, delay action, miss opportunities, persuade, or fail to mobilize followers. Poor decisions or no decisions, when needed, will destroy leadership and trust, while good decisions have a positive, motivational impact. In our sales leader research and training, decision-making has a constant high ranking so we have supported it with a proprietary process and unique tools. Well-calculated decisions can result in achieving sales vision goals, and more important, enhancing your overall image as a strong sales leader.

Decision-making is more than judgment; it often evolves around your risk-taking and action-orientation, both potentially good or bad abilities. Good decisions also save your company money while delayed nondecisions or poor decisions are often very costly. Instinct alone will not work when making typical sales decisions like these (or avoiding them too long!):

- Dealing with sales rep performance problems
- Who to coach and when, what skills or knowledge to focus on
- When to terminate a poor performer
- How to handle customer problems and/or opportunities
- How much risk to take in implementing action plans
- When and how to get around obstacles
- Who to hire when needed to expand or fill an open territory
- When training is needed
- Recommending a purchase, or change in compensation
- How to create and effectively launch a vision strategy for your sales team

If you completed the Vision/Risk Leadership Indicator, you learned about your own decision-making ability along with the influence of risk-taking and timing of your actions. Hopefully, this exercise got your attention. We're now ready to move on to a unique process that will help you make instinctive decisions (minor ones) and enable you to analyze complex situations and make the best possible decision.

ROI Decision-Making Process

Earlier, I defined sales leadership as the ability to positively influence the actions and attitudes of the sales team to achieve or surpass their goals. Part of this influence involves handling a variety of decisions, some important, others minor. As a *sales manager,* you may be making decisions that are ordinarily supported by higher management. As a *sales leader,* you may be faced with decisions on issues that are not fully supported by others or that involve coping with organizational politics.

Decision-making, especially in regard to leadership, isn't always easy, but well-calculated decisions can result in achieving your sales vision goals and in enhancing your overall image as a leader. To make effective decisions and to improve your ability to reach and maintain a solid success ratio, you need a decision-making process. It will help you handle people and customer problems, enable you to carry out your plans, overcome problems, and more. Operating with instinct alone is high risk and dangerous.

The Porter Henry & Co. proven decision process is called ROI. Yet another acronym! ROI reminds the sales leader to assess the three most important issues in every critical decision: Risk, Opportunity, Investment. The three ROI indicators interact and are the most important issues in most decisions. In the following pages, I will explore the process and provide a tool to give you a running start (and winning edge) on every sales leader decision—big, medium, and small.

The ROI Decision Process consists of the following five steps, each of which may take a few thoughtful minutes, or days, depending on its importance or timing.

1. Weigh the Importance of the Decision. Ask yourself how important the decision is. How much of your time, other people's time, money, and energy should be expended on making the decision? The decision may be a simple one that takes a few minutes to go through the process mentally, or could be delayed and time-consuming to allow for research and discussion.

2. Search Relevant Facts and Information. Although this sounds obvious and simple, it is easy to be deficient in completing this step. The natural tendency, and sometimes unavoidable necessity to make quick decisions, can cause the decision-maker to disregard the fact that pertinent information is missing. Once you acknowledge that there are missing facts, you must determine if they're worth finding and if you have the time to invest in searching for them.

Ask yourself the following questions in searching out relevant facts/information:

- What are the criteria for this decision?
- What information do I need?
- Are the missing facts worth finding?
- How much time do I have?

The most effective decisions are made with as many facts and as much time as the decision requires. The answers to these questions will determine when you might have to move a little faster than you normally would, or make the best decision possible with limited information.

For example, if a salesperson were in danger of losing his third account this quarter, you'd probably want to get out there quickly. If you take time to analyze call reports, or talk to other salespeople or customers, you may not be able to help the salesperson maintain his confidence level and you may end up losing even more business. In this case, you may not have all the information up front, but time is of the essence. Collect the facts, including seeing the customer, resolve the problem, and deal with the salesperson later (as a related decision).

3. Identify Decision Options. In this step you want to list *all* of the possible options, before evaluating ideas and selecting one to implement.

- First, write down a list of obvious options.
- Brainstorm creative option additions and add them to your list—be creative without evaluating any of your ideas.
- Combine and enhance options. When you're reviewing your list of creative and obvious options, you may find that you could implement more than one option at a time or build on one of your options.

For example, let's say one of your salespeople has plateaued during the last two months. Two of the options you listed are:

- Counsel her to determine, if possible, why this is happening.
- Work with her extensively in the field, seeking reasons and coaching.

The combined and enhanced option might be to implement both options *and* have her travel with a successful, senior salesperson.

The last part of identifying decision options is to narrow your list down to two or three of the most doable. The only criteria you use are how doable the option is.

4. Use ROI Tool to Compare Options. In the third step of the ROI Decision Process, you compare your most doable options in terms of Risk, Opportunity, and Investment using high, medium, and low rankings.

- *Risk:* The probability of a decision option leading to failure. How likely is it that you will get your desired result with these options? Rank Risk as High, Medium, or Low.

- *Opportunity:* The impact the decision option will have on results. In addition to how well it will solve a problem, consider how it will affect other issues such as sales performance, your team, and your image. Use High, Medium, and Low rankings again.

- *Investment:* The cost of implementing the option. Besides the monetary value involved, each option will require a High, Medium, or Low degree of your time, the sales team's time, other resources, and so on. The total of these other costs can be significant. Be careful not to downplay those costs for options that may rank favorably in risk and opportunity.

For example, let's say you have a new product to launch and communicate to your sales team, and they are located in five states. One of your options is to bring your salespeople into a central location for a one-day meeting or rank the opportunity if covered by phone conference. The travel, meeting, and lodging expenses total $2,000. That does not reflect other costs to the individuals and to the company that may outweigh the obvious and calculable costs, such as:

- Salesperson's time out of the territory, salary, commission
- Lost business as a result of absence from the territory
- Your time and efforts in planning and attending the meeting

Select "Best" Option

The last step in the ROI Decision Process is to select the best option based on your Risk, Opportunity, and Investment rankings. There are four components in selecting the best option as illustrated in the ROI worksheet tool that follows.

ROI Decision Tool

Decision to be made: _____

1. How important is this decision?
   □ High □ Medium □ Low

2. What are the criteria for making the decision?
   • What information do I need?
   • Are missing facts worth finding?
   • How much time do I have to make the decision?

3. What are *all* my options (not just the obvious ones)?
   _____
   _____
   _____
   _____

4. What are the best options? What is the Risk, Opportunity, and Investment for each?

Option 1	Option 2	Option 3
Describe:	Describe:	Describe:
Risk H M L Opportunity H M L Investment H M L	Risk H M L Opportunity H M L Investment H M L	Risk H M L Opportunity H M L Investment H M L

5. Select best option: #_____to implement on timely basis.
   Rationale: _____

Sales Management Success: Optimizing Performance to Build a Powerful Sales Team.

It should be obvious to you that this format can be cumbersome for simple decisions like planning who and when to coach, handling a minor sales/customer problem, or resolving a team dispute. And you're right, but once you start using this process for major problems and decisions, you will use it instinctively (mentally, that is) for almost every problem. Further, the ideal decision, which doesn't always surface, is *High Opportunity, Low Investment, Low Risk. If it doesn't hit this target right on, then the best decision is your judgment based on assessing the three ROIs.* Sometimes, you analysis will lead you to "no decision" and that can be okay in fuzzy situations.

Before I close the door on this segment, I'd like to share some of my personal decision-making rules to supplement those already mentioned. They have been earned and learned the hard way as both sales manager and sales leader.

KURZROCK'S SIMPLE DECISION-MAKING RULES

1. Never ignore or casually postpone a request or problem decision, regardless of the source, even if it sounds minor or unimportant.
2. Timing is always critical even for small or personal decisions. If you can't respond on the spot, indicate specifically when you will make the decision and then answer it on time!
3. Avoid putting off decisions, because few problems solve themselves or get better without leadership. With complex or important decisions, take as much time as needed to assess or determine options, and then evaluate them with the ROI process.
4. When a salesperson brings you a nonsolvable problem or personal issue, thank him or her for bringing it to your attention and indicate (1) why it may not work or why it is not important, or (2) try to modify it and give the salesperson due credit.

———

INFLUENCE

Influence is often associated with sales leadership. It's a broad and far-reaching strategy, almost implemented with instinct. Most actions you take with the sales team (and sometimes without) impact your ongoing influence. For example, many of the previous strategies like motivation, hiring, coaching, and so on will impact your influence with the team and individual salespeople, even if they are not involved.

Influence is affecting the thoughts, motivations, actions, and behaviors of your sales team in a positive manner so they follow you as the sales leader. The definition of sales leadership itself contains the words "positively influence." Influence is critical to you in your role to:

- Keep the sales team on track.
- Have a motivated and united sales team that achieves results.
- Provide overall career direction.
- Offer support in tough times.
- Build participation, involvement, teamwork.
- Deal with individual problems and development.
- Challenge and drive the salesforce.
- Maintain a positive image in the eyes of your sales team.

If you do not have the ability to influence your sales team, then you are not functioning as a leader. As mentioned, almost every action you take and every strategy you launch reflects and impacts influence. However, there are two interacting methods you use almost unconscientiously to influence, and while you probably have mastered them both to a good degree, they deserve mention here to underline their critical role in sales leadership and to remind you of their importance in leading and influencing the sales team. To muddy the waters, communication style and personal abilities overlap to some degree in daily management and with most of the strategies previously discussed. Let's separate and review them individually.

Communication Style

Style is the approach you use in different situations to achieve desired results through your salespeople. For example, your approach may need to be heavy-handed and forceful when discussing sales results. Other situations may require you to be participative and supportive. The challenge is to select the most appropriate style for each situation. On the downside, General Patton's style, characterized by extreme yelling and bad-mouthing at mistakes, may work in war time but will obviously fail in today's business world.

There are four distinct sales leadership styles you can use to influence your sales team. Your ability to identify when each style is appropriate and use each style effectively is critical to your role as a leader.

The four sales leadership styles are directing, selling, participating, and delegating.

Directing. Directing is mostly one-way communication. You tell the salesperson what you want in an autocratic manner. Although directing has a negative connotation when considered in terms of leading or managing, it is appropriate and effective in specific situations. Directing requires confidence in the information you are providing and specificity in delivering it. Use a directing style:

- With new salespeople
- To communicate decisions
- To provide instructions
- To discipline
- At impasses
- When directed from above
- To communicate policy/procedures

Selling. You certainly know selling! Selling is persuading a salesperson or the sales team to move in a particular direction. You attempt to gain commitment by convincing others that what you're saying is true or is the best option. When using the selling style, you give the other party the opportunity to respond.

Use a selling style:

- To introduce a new product/program/service
- To introduce a different selling technique (e.g., selling the appointment versus cold calling)
- To present a new concept, idea, method, or procedure
- To exceed already established sales goals
- To challenge the sales team

Participating. Participating is used to get input, buy-in, feedback, or opinions from the sales team. The participating style encourages two-way communication and an open, honest exchange of ideas. You have an opportunity to access a variety of ideas and to show that you respect and value the input of your sales team. You can enhance their sense of being valuable members of the team.

Use a participating style:

- To get feedback on problems
- To obtain suggestions for improving individual performance or team sales results
- To coach in the field
- To counsel
- To obtain information on the progress with an account and to brainstorm strategies for further development

Delegating. Delegating is empowering salespeople with the freedom to do their jobs or to enhance their personal development. Salespeople who have demonstrated the ability to work successfully and independently often have the confidence to continue to perform with little supervision. This style may be difficult for some sales leaders because you are interested in, concerned about, and feel responsible for all of your salespeople, and want to stay involved. The key to the delegating style is monitoring and follow-up to keep yourself assured of the continued efforts and success on the part of the salesperson, and to allow the salesperson enough room to do the job confidently without feeling you are "checking up." This is the least interactive of the four leadership styles but it has many benefits when used with other strategies. It's essential in autonomy motivation, saves your time so you can manage priorities, and is an important role in sales leadership.

Use a delegating style:

- To empower salespeople for job enrichment, motivation, or challenge
- With successful senior salespeople who have demonstrated abilities and expressed a desire to work independently
- To develop individuals by building their confidence in their own ability to work successfully with little supervision
- In tight time periods
- When someone else can do it better than you or you want someone else's ideas
- When your intervention won't change the situation

Although each sales leadership style is separate and distinct from the others, you will find that many situations require more than one style. For example, in a sales meeting you may need to use the selling style to introduce a new product, and follow that with the participating style to get ideas on how to launch the new product. You need to be flexible within situations as well as from situations to situations. The more flexible you are, the greater your ability will be to communicate to people and influence their behavior in the desired direction.

Personal Abilities

The impact of personal abilities is different from that of abilities needed to launch or drive a strategy. Personal abilities refer to what you are, whereas the other forces refer to what you do. The overall perception of your characteristics, traits, and personality makes a composite picture of your image as a sales leader. A positive image will gain the trust, confidence, and respect of your sales team that will encourage them to follow you. That's influence.

Personal abilities are personality and behavior characteristics that are difficult to measure because they are subjective. Their identification and intensity rely on individual perceptions.

These characteristics are also difficult to change and develop. Modifications can only occur over a period of time and require the desire and commitment to make changes. Following are 10 accepted characteristics or personal abilities of sales leaders, which you can use as a personal checklist:

1. A good role model
2. Sincere and open personality
3. Pride and passion for doing an effective job
4. Integrity
5. High energy and endurance
6. Enthusiastic and optimistic
7. Has team's confidence, trust, respect
8. Has empathy
9. Gets involved, works with team to make it successful
10. Has strong management, leadership, and selling skills

When Porter Henry & Co. first introduced our Sales Leadership workshop, we piloted it with a partner company, a major manufacturer. One of the tools was a pre-workshop assessment, a 360-degree survey for each sales manager. It contained 40 assessment questions on leadership abilities, which was submitted confidentially by the sales manager (self-assessment), the sales team, and the sales manager's boss. The data was computed into a report, averaging and comparing the 40 assessments from the three sources and given confidentially to each sales manager early in the workshop to set learning objectives. During the workshop, I noticed that one sales manager, who it turned out was one of the top producers, seemed angry and annoyed with little positive participation throughout the two-day workshop. Later, in follow-up conversations with the client, I learned the cause: he had received very low grades anonymously from the sales team, specifically negative ratings on "trust and respect " and "open personality," although he had high marks on everything else. The client asked me to call him after the workshop to calm him down, explain the rating format, and how this poor feedback could happen. By then, he was feeling better and more rational, and indicated that he probably created the low grade himself because he spent so much time working, less time with the team, and literally ignored attention to individuals unless they had a problem. He indicated he would work on it and true to his promise, six months later when we did the same follow-up survey, he got good ratings in every one of the 40 behavior questions.

Recognition of development needs is the first step, and challenging for most of us. Obviously, we all have these capabilities but may not use them frequently, or always put the best foot forward. Some may not be pursued at all. Once a shortfall is identified, the next step is to develop a simple action plan, relatively long range to improve it with daily focus. It is not always easy to think of actions you can take to develop or change your behavior. Be as creative and open as possible. Seek ideas from others. Perhaps you should discuss your development needs with your boss. At a minimum, try to catch yourself when you're doing something that reflects one of the behaviors you'd like to change. Make note of what you say or do and commit to doing it differently next time.

As you look at yourself in the behavior mirror (internally, that is) and recognize a personal behavior that can be improved, work to improve it over time. Use our 10 behaviors as a checklist review, so you can feel confident that they are enhancing your sales leadership development, and none of the behaviors are retarding it. Like all strategies, your style and personal behavior need individual development goals that only you can you can determine, along with a strategy of awareness and improvement.

————

Congratulations on reading this book, and I trust you've gotten some super ideas to help you innovate and accelerate your sales manager/sales leader career using the eight turbo-charged strategies as a driving force. However, you have only completed the "reading" marathon and this experience will help you master appropriate strategies; it is just the beginning of your real-life sales leadership career path. I'm reminded of this frequently by a framed picture one of my daughters gave me. It's a photo of a runner jogging near a lake and woods with the title beneath it: "There is no finish line." Continuous improvement is vital for every effective sales manager/leader with new learning and forward steps to meet dynamic challenges like technology, economy, the marketplace, and leading new challenging generations of salespeople.

This book has provided you with a foundation for eight turbo-charged strategies, all vital and overlapping, along with a collection of skills/abilities to drive each one. Learning and application are your challenges. I hope you capitalize further on the Porter Henry & Company strategies/knowledge/skills and my career experiences, and employ the Toolbox that follows in Chapter 10, in leading your sales team to great success. The content serves as a source for developing your strategies, skills, behavior, and abilities that you can reference when challenged or needed. My best wishes for a successful and dynamic sales manager/sales leader career!

10

Your Turbo-Charged Strategic Toolbox

This chapter rounds up most of the worksheets that appear in the preceding chapters and provides a brief explanation on how to use them.

ALIGNING AND ENHANCING SALES MOTIVATION

No sales manager directly motivates salespeople to sell more. Yet, the effective manager can align, enhance, and even awaken an individual's intrinsic motivation. While all salespeople are motivated to sell (at varying levels and direction), each person has different motivations; often hidden, they can be detected over time.

Thanks to Dan Pink's research shared in his best-selling book *DRiVE*, two of today's priority motivations have surfaced; Mastery (motivation to improve performance) and Autonomy (desire to work alone on a challenging issue, idea, or project). Both are business- and job-related, and relevant to many salespeople. However, they need to be awakened in salespeople—the sales manager's job. The tools enhance and support these individual motivations to provide support and to stay on track. Ideally, they should be subtly offered to the sales team for individual choices in gaining skills, development, and accomplishment.

My Skill Mastery Tool

My Mastery Tool for Improved Performance provides an individual with a step-by-step, measurable plan for self-improvement. While many salespeople want to improve (master skills and job), they seldom know how to do it on their own beyond the sales manager's coaching (if and when available). The Mastery Tool provides a personal, individual application guide for practice and follow-up self-coaching. It enables the mastery-motivated sales rep to identify and plan sales calls where he can use and practice skill development.

A minimum of six sales calls are needed to reinforce a skill so the salesperson literally "owns" her personal development. The tool targets one skill at a time, the only way to practice and develop successfully. Another column is used to rank the skill performance 1–10 on each sales call so she can see improvement and gain reinforcement. A final column is for notes.

This is a great tool for any salesperson who is motivated strongly to improve, and it provides a professional track for focusing on one skill until improved. That's mastery fulfilled! Constant practice over time is key.

My Mastery Tool for Improved Performance

Describe targeted skill: _____

Select minimum six sales calls (within one to two weeks); repeat cycle?	1–10 skill ranking for each skill performance	Notes on skill performance, improvements	Notes on sales call overall, account follow-up
1.			
2.			
3.			
4.			
5.			
6.			
7.			
8.			
9.			
10.			
11.			
12.			
Month's Analysis: # calls skill used: Improved? Not satisfied? Repeat cycle on same skill? Add new skill?	**Average Score:**	**Summary Notes:**	**Next Mastery Steps:**

Sales Management Success: Optimizing Performance to Build a Powerful Sales Team.

Next Mastery Steps: Check via sales manager coaching, reinforce with role-play, outside courses, and learning; review skill when planning; move Mastery focus to a new target skill when you have mastered targeted skill.

My Autonomy Challenge Plan

My Autonomy Challenge Plan is designed for salespeople who are motivated to *accomplish more on their own*. While all salespeople are responsible for some autonomy in managing a territory or specific accounts, some salespeople want more autonomy, individually handling a special project or challenge.

Autonomy is not for everyone, but many of today's salespeople are motivated by their ideas and further accomplishment, reaching for individual recognition and growth. This is not for every salesperson, but for those who "volunteer" and succeed, it rewards the salesperson with achievement and development, and provides benefits for the sales manager and sales team, as well.

My Autonomy Challenge Plan

Planning steps	Details on implementing the situation task
1. Situation (what type of improvement, solution, new ideas anticipated)	Task Objective:
2. Time (consider time on and off the job and ETC)	Expected Time for Completion (ETC): % of Sales Time Required:
3. Action (techniques or methods)	Description of How Accomplished:
4. Result (potential value of this effort)	Anticipated Accomplishment:
5. Team (possible benefits to teammates and how best to communicate)	Communicate Results to Sales Team: __Sales meeting __Telephone conference, Skype __Email feedback __Other:
Signed approval by both sales manager and salesperson:	Date:

Typical autonomy plans initiated by either the salesperson or sales manager might include challenges like: coaching new salespeople or acting as a mentor, testing a new product, identifying new product applications, researching new customers' potential, and so on. The key is that both the sales manager and autonomy-driven salesperson must agree on the five essential elements in the plan as noted on the tool: *Situation* (task), *Time* (allocated/completion date), *Actions* employed, potential *Result*, and *Team* benefits/feedback so everyone gains.

Once established, the salesperson is on his own with a few critical guidelines and support from the sales manager. In the solution process, she develops skills, gains knowledge and new abilities, and enhances sales performance.

COUNSELING TO IMPROVE SALES PERFORMANCE

Sales counseling, in its simplest form, is meeting with a salesperson in private to discuss her performance. Good performance should be reviewed periodically with everyone since most salespeople are hungry for feedback. On the other hand, when a salesperson fails to improve over time, has a problem that can't be corrected by coaching, or has poor behavior or conduct, it's time for private, confidential counseling. Hopefully, counseling will surface the cause, if possible, and create behavior change. The counseling tools are designed for delivering this message, getting feedback, creating agreement, and launching a successful action plan.

Counseling Planning Tool

The Counseling Planning Tool is your playbook for planning and implementing this important and sensitive strategy in a fail-safe manner.

Step 1 enables you to open the conversation in a positive way, while stating your goal. It is critical to set the stage for a positive session.

Step 2 suggests you wait for a positive response. If not forthcoming, probe for any resistance or possible causes.

Step 3 is for implementing a solution, so plan your questions to learn about solutions, test ideas, check his attitude for change, and determine a plan.

Step 4 nails down the salesperson's commitment for the agreed-upon solution.

Counseling Planning Tool

Critical steps	Sales manager's actions	Salesperson's responses/ notes
1. Open the session. • State problem behaviors • Express concern • Compare to expectations, past positive performance • Purpose/desired results		
2. Wait for positive response. If not forthcoming, probe for resistance, determine causes.		
3. Plan questions to seek and/or to offer solutions, and ultimately determine one.		
4. Gain commitment on solutions.		
5. Establish follow-up (when, how).		
6. Create a joint action plan in writing using the following Action Plan.		
7. Close session on a positive note.		

Step 5 is to develop a joint plan so the salesperson understands that you both will work together, and you will be checking actions for improvement.

Step 6 requires a detailed action plan in writing.

Step 7 is a reminder to close the session on a positive note.

Use this tool for planning and executing your counseling session, and for taking notes. Most important, save it for any repeat sessions and legal protection.

Sales Improvement Action Plan

The Sales Improvement Action Plan is critical and should be part of most counseling sessions to guarantee action. Completed jointly, in concert with a counseling session, it starts with a specific, realistic goal, including dates for completion of appropriate steps. Each step should have a target date for achievement, your support as sales manager, and improvements. Keep a copy with notes in the event future action is required.

Sales Improvement Action Plan

Salesperson: _____ **Date:** _____

SMART Goal: _____

Action steps	Target date	Sales manager support	Performance improvements

Sales Management Success: Optimizing Performance to Build a Powerful Sales Team.

MANAGING SALES PERFORMANCE

Managing sales performance is one of the sales manager's greatest challenges, and in order to do it effectively and efficiently, you need a strategy and a strategic action tool to make it work. Understanding and following the model is the first step, and it is visualized in the tool itself. The model and tool together enable four interacting steps, which are necessary to monitor the performance of each sales rep on a quarterly basis, taking appropriate actions if needed to correct or reinforce performance. The four steps in the model are:

1. Monitor critical success factors (tool and model list 10 essential ones).
2. Identify performance gains/gaps (model indicates four key skills/actions for each success factor).
3. Determine causes (attitude, skill shortfall, not understanding expectations, etc.) that often point to right action/solution.
4. Take appropriate action(s) when needed from list of 10 sales manager options.

Review the Managing Sales Performance model provided in the tool before proceeding to the explanation of the tracking tool (Figure 10.1).

Sales Performance Plan

The Sales Performance Plan dovetails with the model and provides a tracking tool for each salesperson along with sales manager actions when called for. The tool is a composite place to add notes, observations, and coaching experience so you can document them for analysis and action, if required.

The first column (*Success Factors*) is a checklist of the key sales performance skills/actions that impact performance. This enables the sales manager to zero in on the skills and actions that drive sales performance.

The second column (*Expectations*) helps you focus on your goals and objectives (also communicated to each salesperson) by listing the expectations themselves or updated notes.

The third column (*Gains/Gaps*) is for spotting improvements that get reinforced and shortfalls in performance that may need correcting.

Sales Performance Plan for: _____

Qtr: _____

Success factors	Expectations	Gains/gaps	Facts/metrics	Possible cause(s)	Manager actions	Results/next teps
Account penetration						
Administration						
Contact activity						
General behavior						
New business						
Product mix						
Sales volume						
Selling skills						
Strategy execution						
Territory management						

Sales Management Success: Optimizing Performance to Build a Powerful Sales Team.

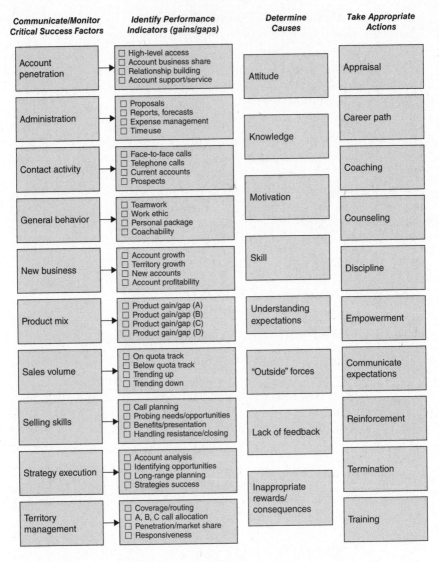

Figure 10.1   Sales Performance System

The fourth column (*Facts/Metrics*) is where you add numbers if possible to reinforce your analysis and help determine solutions.

The fifth column (*Possible Cause(s)*) is for determining a possible cause. If so, it will often point to one of the 10 actions listed in the model.

The sixth column (Manager Actions) is to note any of the 10 actions (or others) that you implement to reinforce or upgrade performance.

The last column (Results/Next Steps) is used to track changes in performance and indicate continuity for the next quarter's Sales Performance Plan. It should be obvious that you do not need to act on every issue, but when a salesperson has a number of gaps (even in different success factors), it's time to take action.

Sharing individual plans with each salesperson at the end of the quarter is desirable and will gain respect for your leadership ability and transparency.

This strategy, when used correctly and implemented on an ongoing quarterly basis for each salesperson, provides many benefits. It will enable you to identify and surface weaknesses *before* they become problems, help you manage your time, focus on your sales performance priorities, and generate sales results for your sales team.

———

MANAGING TIME TO ACHIEVE PRIORITIES

In the sales manager's world, time allocation is often ruled by interruptions from salespeople, customers, bosses, emergencies, travel, and pet interests like email and personal selling. Recognize that time management and related performance is a huge challenge for today's sales managers. Often with 15–20 defined activities such as coaching, supervising, training, hiring, forecasting, managing a team of different, and anxious salespeople, the job has dysfunctional potential. Add in Type A bosses with emergencies, and a mix of customer problems. Guess what? Time management becomes an ongoing, never-ending challenge that needs to be corralled.

While effective time management leads to greater efficiency and ongoing good habits, the real payback strategy is allocating time so that your top priorities get sufficient time for successful completion. This can only be accomplished by (1) learning where your time is now being spent, (2) identifying and ranking your priorities, (3) reallocating your time to insure that top priorities have enough time to exceed expectations, and (4) using professional time management techniques to control time-killers.

Sales Manager Time Allocation Tool

Sales Manager Time Allocation is a strategy for insuring that your major priorities get sufficient time for completion.

The first column, *Sales Manager Activities*, is a list of typical sales manager activities that require time. You can add others if needed.

Next, you should rank your priorities in the second column, *Priority*, as indicated, by A, B, and C. Based on Pareto's Principle of the "important few, and unimportant many," we recommend three A priorities, four B priorities, and the balance ranked as Cs, based only on their importance to your job success.

Next, you need to determine where your time is currently being spent and this can be realistically accomplished by doing a one- or two-week study of your time activity. We recommend you track your daily time, using columns *Monday–Friday*, and insert a check mark for each approximate 30 minutes used for appropriate activities.

When the one- or two-week time study is completed, you will be able to total the hours spent for each activity in the *Total Hours* column.

Before the final step, it's a good idea to convert the hours to percentages in the % of Time column to facilitate the analysis for reallocating your time.

Once this step is completed, the final step is reallocating your time for optimum performance. It requires that you use the last column, *Ideal Time*, to update your future time allocations:

1. Allocate sufficient time to accomplish your A priorities.
2. Make sure that your B priorities get enough time for completion.
3. Spread the remaining time percentage among the many C activities as needed.

When finished, you will have your personal time allocation (target) for future use and the discipline to follow it in a reasonable fashion for optimum performance. To accommodate changes, this strategy should be adjusted yearly by repeating each step from a new time study to reallocating your time for priorities. It's also imperative to manage your daily time by using time saving techniques like detailed planning of each day's activity, establishing routines, setting time limits for activities, and more.

Sales Manager Time Allocation Tool

Sales Manager Activities	Priority A, B, C	Mon.	Tues.	Wed.	Thur.	Fri.	Total Hours	% of Time	Ideal Time %
Administration: general paper/computer work									
Coaching: in field, phone, online									
Company Meetings: attend live, online									
Counseling: individual sales rep problems									
Forecasting: discussion, analysis, review									
Interviewing/Selection: related to hiring									
Management Reports: internal/external									
Managing Sales Team: supervise, communicate									
Marketing: promotions, related activities									
Personal Development: study, review, research									
Planning: strategy, idea generation, future plans									
Sales Meetings: group sessions, live/telephone									
Proposal Writing: help reps, develop input									
Selling: live or phone, with/without rep									
Telephone/Email: sending or receiving, responding									
Training: directing in office									
Travel: include travel done in work hours only									
Other Key Activities:									
TOTALS	XXXXX							100%	

SALES COACHING

According to experts, sales coaching is the most important sales manager strategy. In every situation, sales coaching tools become vital checklists, feedback instruments, and guides for coaching sales calls (often a series with the same salesperson), coaching both skills and account strategy. Effective sales managers must accurately analyze each coaching call's performance, use a proven coaching process afterward, summarize performance gains/gaps at the end of the day or series, and establish plans for ongoing development.

The tools help to accomplish these tactical and strategic goals and enable the sales manager to avoid coaching traps like: failing to reinforce skill improvements, over-coaching with little input from salesperson, coaching the wrong skill, and attempting to cover too much in one coaching conference.

Due to multiple priorities and responsibilities and enlarged sales teams, studies find that field coaching time has been limited to about 10% of the sales manager's activity; it is not enough to provide necessary coaching and reinforcement. This has given rise to virtual coaching, acting as a "frequency" partner to enable adequate coaching. Field coaching establishes a foundation for future development while reinforcing skills. It also sets the stage for virtual sales coaching, so together, the dynamic duo seamlessly increase coaching feedback, frequency, and reinforcement.

Field Sales Coaching Tool

The Field Sales Coaching Tool is designed for both planning and execution, including pre-call discussion and postcall coaching, enhancing observation with notes. It also offers a coaching process for use after each sales call. The effective coaching process must start with an objective (focus on one or more skills), and a pre-call briefing with the salesperson, who should have planned the call. The coaching guide covers these important steps:

- *Coaching objective:* Prior to coaching, you both agree on skill to improve.
- *Pre-call briefing:* Important to determine roles, get briefing, do pre-call coaching.
- *Skill to reinforce:* Observing sales call often identifies improvement to reinforce.

Field Sales Coaching Tool

Salesperson: _____

Account: _____ *Coaching Date:* _____

Coaching based on observation	Sales call coaching notes	Salesperson actions/reactions
Coaching objective:		
Pre-call briefing:		
Skill to reinforce:		
Skill to improve:		
Key observations: 1. 2.		
Coaching process: • Reinforce positive skills/behavior • Have salesperson analyze call first • Use leading questions to highlight weakness • Suggest better way after discussing weak skill • Elicit feedback to check understanding • Encourage practice • Get commitment to improve		
Next steps in account follow-up, development, strategy, pipeline		

- *Skill to improve:* Primary focus for coaching; another may surface in sales call.
- *Key observations:* Supporting issues observed in general, but avoid over-coaching.
- *Coaching process:* A proven process; change sequence to avoid being redundant!
- *Next steps:* Discuss, determine ideas for account penetration and follow-up strategy.

Virtual Sales Coaching Tool

The Virtual Sales Coaching Tool enables the sales manager to coach from anywhere, any time, and coupled with field coaching, dramatically

Virtual Sales Coaching Tool (Postcall Analysis)

Salesperson: _____

Account: _____

Decision-maker: _____

Sales call date: _____

Target skill(s): _____

Sales call analysis	Responses
My sales call objective:	Achieved: Yes No Comments:
If not, why not?	
How well did I execute my target skill(s)?	
What was the most effective element of my sales presentation?	
What could I have done differently or better on this sales call?	
What did I learn that I can use on other sales calls with this account?	
My biggest obstacle in this sales call and what I did to handle it:	
What ideas did I gain that I can use with other accounts?	
Next steps or strategy for this account?	

My earliest date and time to meet with you by phone:

Sales Management Success: Optimizing Performance to Build a Powerful Sales Team.

increases coaching frequency. The salesperson must be cautioned about consistent objectivity and completing it immediately after the sales call. The tool is self-explanatory and the key for accurate coaching. It enables the sales manager and salesperson to plan coaching ASAP, analyze the data, determine questions, and eventually, coach by phone. Ideally, virtual coaching should be employed in a series of six sales calls (during a few weeks) to gain proper reinforcement from the coaching. A virtual coaching series often follows a field visit that establishes a foundation, and sometimes it is desirable to conduct a number of virtual coaching series with a salesperson before a follow-up field visit to validate improvements.

SALES LEADERSHIP

Sales management is different from sales leadership. The major difference is that many sales managers focus on short-term, day-to-day challenges, but the most successful ones eventually become sales leaders shifting toward a more long-term management role.

Leading the sales team long-term requires more planning and analysis to support sales team motivation and performance. Sales leadership, as a strategy, requires tools to perform and impact performance, as well as a strong "batting average" for making the right decisions. The tools below are vital and interactive for sales leaders.

VisiPlan Tool

VisiPlan is a strategic planning tool that is used to generate and launch periodic sales team strategies based on opportunities. The opportunities trigger the strategy or campaign based on the sales manager's vision and ability to look ahead. Once an opportunity is defined, the planning, often including sales team input, is accomplished. Implementation, normally about 6–12 months, is driven by the strategy along with the sales manager's constant communication and feedback on performance.

Done effectively, the strategy provides sales team challenge, motivation, teamwork, and results. However, everything is triggered by the sales leader's vision, or the ability to look ahead constantly, analyze the market, and seek a timely opportunity to create and drive sales team goals, such as: achieve company product mix goals 50-25-25% for the fiscal year; increase division market share 10% within six months; acquire 10 new accounts, in $20K range, during Q1 and Q2.

Visiplan

Date: _____

Vision

Where do you want your sales team to be or go?

Goals

What will you need to achieve to get there? Make the goals SMART:
specific, measurable, aligned, realistic, time-bound

Strategies

How will you achieve your goals? What is your overall approach?

Tactics

For each strategy, what actions need to be taken, by whom, and by when?
Use a separate Tactical Action Plan form for each strategy.

Tactical Action Plan
Strategy (from Visiplan):

Action Steps	Who	Target date

The planning is made easy by the tool, which requires: Vision, Goals, Strategies, and Tactics. It includes individual sales team (and others') responsibilities, with suitable timelines for accomplishment, strong oversight, and constant communication and reinforcement from the sales leader.

ROI Decision Tool

The ROI Decision Tool is vital for important decisions. Decision-making is critical for both sales managers and sales leaders in terms of their performance, reputation, and respect from the sales team. The tool initially requires creativity to identify multiple solutions or options for a problem, challenge, or complex decision. Examples of serious decisions are hiring/terminating, territory expansion or assignment, who to focus your coaching on, how to handle a salesperson's performance problem, and so on.

The bottom line of the decision tool is comparing/ranking two or three of the best options on the ROI format (Risk, Opportunity, Investment) so you can identify the best one and make the right decision. That's where the ranking comes in to play: High, Medium, Low.

The ideal decision (seldom available) is Low Risk, High Opportunity, Low Investment. In most cases, the best decision is the one closest to this perfect model.

In every situation, using this tool and process mandate analysis and thinking, and eliminates "shooting from the hip" on important decisions, or making bad choices on instinct alone. Once the sales manager learns to follow this tool, he will mentally cover the three ROI criteria for minor decisions.

ROI Decision Tool

Decision to be made: _____

1. How important is this decision?
   ☐ High ☐ Medium ☐ Low

2. What are the criteria for making the decision?
   - What information do I need?
   - Are missing facts worth finding?
   - How much time do I have to make the decision?

3. What are *all* my options (not just the obvious ones)?

   _____

   _____

   _____

   _____

   _____

4. What are the best options? What is the Risk, Opportunity, and Investment for each?

Option 1	Option 2	Option 3
Describe:	Describe:	Describe:
Risk H M L	Risk H M L	Risk H M L
Opportunity H M L	Opportunity H M L	Opportunity H M L
Investment H M L	Investment H M L	Investment H M L

5. Select best option: #_____ to implement on timely basis.
   Rationale: _____

SELECTING FUTURE SALES STARS

Sales managers are frequently challenged to hire the right person, but based on the high turnover in most salesforces, hiring is much less than perfect. At an estimated $250,000 cost (includes salary, training, manager's time, and so on) for each replacement, it is highly desirable to improve both the hiring process and overall strategy. Sales managers often fail to ask the right questions, or dig deep into qualifications and skills, and that's where the breakdowns occur.

The best method is to ask the right questions, identify behavior strengths and weaknesses, and ultimately, compare candidates' qualities on all the critical skills, behaviors, and experience. The ideal way to probe behaviors like work ethic and sales motivation level is using a tool to surface deep answers and experience.

The four step STAR questioning process is ideal. A final decision matrix is also required. The decision matrix lists the key performance requirements for salespeople and offers a ranking system to add a degree of objectivity to the final selection. It enables the sales manager to review all the candidates on one page, seeking the one with the top score, and therefore with the best chances of success in the job. Once completed, it also serves as a document for HR or your management to justify the selection and win support from others.

STAR Behavior Questioning Tool

The STAR Behavior Questioning Tool is ideal for in-depth questioning of sensitive behaviors that are normally difficult to assess in an interview. Included as important for salespeople are: motivation level, hard work, integrity, resiliency, competitiveness, enthusiasm, and many others. While some may be apparent in an interview, others may be hidden.

The four-step *STAR* questions, *Situation, Task, Action, Result,* will normally trigger a complete, in-depth, and accurate response so you can add it into your decision format. Because of the many sales jobs and different expectations, and the difficulty in measuring behavior, this tool should be used to surface the three or four key behaviors required for success that are not fully determined by normal interview questions and accompanying responses.

Star Behavior Questioning Tool

Candidate: _____ *Date:* _____

Star questions	Candidate responses
BEHAVIOR 1:	
Situation:	
Task:	
Action:	
Result:	
BEHAVIOR 2:	
Situation:	
Task:	
Action:	
Result:	

Star questions	Candidate responses
BEHAVIOR 3:	
Situation:	
Task:	
Action:	
Result:	

Sales Management Success: Optimizing Performance to Build a Powerful Sales Team.
Copyright © 2019 by Warren Kurzrock. All rights reserved.

Best Candidate Selection Matrix

The Best Candidate Decision Matrix should be the final tool used in the hiring process because it covers all the elements of the "ideal salesperson." The ranking for each person on the various in-depth values, 1–10, makes it easy to determine the candidate with the highest score.

While it is easy to use the tool, your challenge is making sure you have an assessment for each of the five factors and the 12 performance issues. Some, such as education and work experience factors, are easy to compare, but ranking the sales performance issues will challenge you to do a totally in-depth job of questioning.

If you can't answer or rank any of these issues with confidence, it's time to back up and conduct more assessments before using this tool to finalize your decision. No salesperson will get a total of 10 on every issue, and some issues may not be important. You can certainly add others specific to your company or territory.

The key is (1) doing your homework during the interviews: validation of talents with repetitive and in-depth questions, checking references, skill performance in role-play, and so on, and (2) selecting the person with the highest score, assuming she has no significant gaps among the 17 factors/performance issues.

Best Candidate Decision Matrix

Use this guide to compare candidates and make the best selection. Rate each candidate: 10 = highest; 5 = medium; 1 = lowest on a scale of 1–10.

Candidates comparison:	1.	2.	3.	4.
Factors:				
Education				
Work experience				
Performance				
Skills/knowledge				
Personal qualities, behavior				
How well each candidate will be able to:				
Deliver sales presentations.				
Build, sustain relationships.				
Meet or exceed goals/sales plan.				
Deal with customers.				
Plan territory coverage.				
Care for/use company materials/equipment.				
Develop knowledge and skills.				
Prospect for new business.				
Be flexible, accept coaching and change.				
Follow instructions.				
Get along with other reps in business unit.				
Be honest/systematic: expenses reports.				
Totals				

ACKNOWLEDGMENTS

THIS BOOK COULD NOT HAVE BEEN written without the sales training experiences, research, creativity, and learning provided to me by countless people and organizations over many years. I am grateful to everyone who knowingly or unknowingly shared ideas and content that have enabled me to capture, combine, refine, and enhance their input in *Sales Management Success*. I sincerely dedicate the book's creation to all contributors and to current and future sales managers who employ the strategies to achieve excellence and greater success. The key contributors who I would like to recognize are:

Porter Henry Jr. founded our company. Now deceased, he was my mentor for 10 years. A sales training genius and perfectionist, he passed on his research and knowledge for salesforce development. This foundation enabled us to grow the company and ultimately develop a world-class curriculum of today's 30 world-class sales and sales management courses and strategies.

William Voelkel, who joined Porter Henry & Co. as a project manager early on and grew to become creative director and eventually president, is an active partner today. A great sales trainer and designer, Will supervised and helped create much of the Porter Henry curriculum and strategies, along with multiple custom projects for clients, generating new ideas with each challenge.

150 sponsor companies, in groups of 6–10 sales trainers, partnered with Porter Henry & Co. to fund, develop, and validate each off-the-shelf course; shared best practices; acted as critics; and validated the training with their sales teams.

Thousands of clients over the years who used our products to train salespeople and sales managers and provided invaluable feedback for continuous updating and improvement of our curriculum.

As author, I have participated, witnessed, and retained much of their shared knowledge, skills, and experiences. Consequently, I dedicate the book to everyone above, and I thank them for sharing their wealth of information so I could transform the high points into a professional guidebook with a life of its own.

ABOUT THE AUTHOR

A MEMBER OF THE PORTER HENRY & COMPANY STAFF for over 25 years, Warren Kurzrock became president in 1985, and CEO in 1995. He has comprehensive experience in every facet of development, including needs analysis, training, sales manager/leader performance, custom project design, strategy, and long-range planning. After U.S. Navy service, Warren started his sales career with Republic Steel Company. He then joined Transcopy Corporation, progressing quickly from a top sales representative to branch manager, regional manager, and then to division manager. In his last assignment before resigning, he built the largest and most profitable division in the company, managing a team of four sales managers and over 40 salespeople.

Warren was a pioneer member of the Professional Society for Sales & Marketing Training, ASTD, and the Instructional Systems Association, and is a frequent speaker at conventions and national sales meetings. He has published articles in *Training* magazine, co-authored a classic article for Harvard Business Review entitled Manage Your Salesforce as a System and *Sales and Marketing Management*. Warren also authored an award-winning book, *The Sales Strategist: 6 Breakthrough Strategies to*

Win New Business. He holds a BA from Duke University and an MBA in marketing from the New York University Graduate School of Business.

As CEO, Warren has transformed Porter Henry & Co. into a global company with 30 proprietary workshops for salespeople and sales managers and 18 online courses on the Illumeo.com website. Warren and the Porter Henry team have produced results in hundreds of sales and sales manager development assignments for clients, big and small, including Pepsi-Cola, NAPA, Dannon Yogurt, Chubb Insurance, Schneider Electric, Tumi, Nabisco, Novartis, John Wiley & Sons, W.W. Grainger, MicroStrategy, and many others.

INDEX